CHANNEL PASSAGE

CHANNEL PASSAGE

*The area around Portishead,
Clevedon, Weston-super-Mare
and Burnham-on-Sea*

With 117 illustrations

PAUL NEWMAN

KINGSMEAD PRESS

© PAUL NEWMAN

First Published in 1976 by Kingsmead Press
Rosewell House, Kingsmead Square, Bath
SBN 901571 74 1

Text set in 11 pt Photon Times, printed by photolithography,
and bound in Great Britain at The Pitman Press, Bath

CONTENTS

Map .... facing page 1

Illustrations .... between pages 22, 23; 38, 39; 70, 71; 86 and 87

Acknowledgments vi

Introduction vii

1 Portishead 1
2 Clevedon 10
3 Walton Saint Mary's and the Gordano Valley 19
4 The Northern Levels 28
5 Woodspring 38
6 Weston-super-Mare 45
7 Uphill, Bleadon, Lympsham and Brent Knoll 58
8 The Totts—Brean to Berrow 66
9 Burnham-on-Sea 76
10 The Holms 90

Appendices
11 Essay: A Victorian health resort, growth and decline 93
12 Topographical summaries and other data: The Mendips, Exmoor, Geological Notes, etc. 103
13 List of Follies, Oddities, etc. 106
14 A Literary Note 117
15 Bibliography 125
   Index 127

ACKNOWLEDGMENTS

In the preparation of this work, I would like to thank my uncle, Douglas Hewett, for loaning me his scrapbook of newspaper cuttings, Mr Winston Thomas, the authority on Burnham and Highbridge, and, finally, Mr David Bromwich, of Taunton Local History Library, for arranging the transfer of rare books.

The photographs in this volume are my own, with the single exception of the Nornen figurehead plate, which is the copyright of Mr Melbourne Loynd, a professional photographer of Burnham and Highbridge. The drawings in the text are the work of Miss J. M. Moss.

INTRODUCTION—
THE BRISTOL CHANNEL

THE Bristol Channel is the most prominent feature of the English coastline: a huge tapering indentation with swift tidal streams which, in the midstream, ebb and flow at speeds varying between 6 and 12 miles per hour; and it is calculated that, at any given moment, they contain 700,000 tons of mud held in suspension. Tidal ranges are dramatic: Portishead, at ordinary springs, records tides of up to 44 feet with 31 feet at Neaps. This is only exceeded by those of the Bay of Fundy which shows a maximum difference of 53 feet. Freak tides on the Welsh side of the coast have produced some incredible figures, and there is an entry in an old Kelly's Directory recording a rise of 70 feet—though this may have been a misprint.

Owing to the shifting and accumulation of sediment, the surface features of the Channel are prone to sudden change. Sand and mudbanks build up, are dredged for commercial exploitation, or transported by tidal flow to other parts of the shore. Seaside resorts and beaches are liable to lose their sand, and harbours and piers tend to silt up. As the County Planning Department observed—'The whole regime of the estuary is delicately balanced, thus banks and channels are seldom constant and can easily be altered by new construction work up or downstream.'

Some two thousand years ago, the situation was even more unstable. In fact, at the start of the Christian Era, such places as Glastonbury, Wedmore and Pawlett stood as islands among the vast reed-swamps and saltings. The Saxons and the Normans designed sea-banks—which have been maintained ever since—to check the sprawling tides; and by assiduous drainage and cultivation, vast tracts of low-lying land were reclaimed and made habitable.

Yet, despite such precautions, the land was still subject to extensive and destructive floodings, one of the most calamitous of which occurred in January 1607 when the whole of the Brue Level was submerged:

> In a short tyme did whole villages stand like Islands (compassed round with Waters) and in a short tyme were those Islands undiscoverable, and no where to be found. The tops of trees and houses onely appeared (especially where the Countrey lay lowe) as if at the beginning of the world townes had been built at the bottome of the Sea, and the people had plaide the husbandmen under the waters.*

These violent inundations spoilt the herbage for cattle, produced offensive smells, and, according to John Rutter, made the younger members of the community prone to attacks of ague. Although that last factor is medically uncorroborated, it may be confidently stated that the imminent threat of floodwater, the wearisome struggle against the sea, the constant digging-out of drainage channels and maintenance of sea-walls, left its mark upon the Somerset character. Whether it inbred a sort of dogged grappling tenaciousness, or an air of pessimistic resignation, is a point psychologists may care to debate.

By the close of the nineteenth century, however, all the drainage districts of Somerset had been mapped, the existing outlets enlarged and improved, pumping stations and relief channels firmly established, and fears of flooding allayed, if not eliminated. In the meantime, society had become aware of the great medicinal benefits to be derived from immersing one's body in cold muddy water, and bathing machines,† hefty as caravans, had been set up in the bays and sheltered inlets of the Channel, with awnings that could be raised or lowered, to conceal naked legs, ankles and toes. From as early as 1830, the small towns along the estuary had begun to enjoy a new prosperity.

> George III went to Weymouth, the Prince Regent to Brighton, and the Victorian seaside resorts sprang up on every coast. Inland spas, like Bath and Jacob's Wells, declined. Weston became proudly 'super mare', and Clevedon and Portishead both discovered the value of their beaches instead of hiding behind their protecting hills as they used to. (Eve Wigan)

Scenically, apart from the headlands at Worle, Brean and Middle Hope, the coastline is flat and undramatic—but it has certain physical features of outstanding scientific interest. There is a belt of sand dunes between Burnham and Brean extending for about 7 miles. Locally referred to as 'The Totts', this area is characterised by 'blown sand allus shiften and blowin'' and a thick crop of marram grass which acts as a stabilising agent.

Saltmarshes occur at the mouths of the rivers Axe, Brue, Parret, Yeo and smaller streams. Elaborate canalisation techniques enable the tidal silt to be carried further upstream than formerly, and there is always a great deal of it in evidence at low tide. This attracts large numbers of sea birds for whom the mud flats provide a feeding ground.

---

* From a 1607 tract entitled, 'A true report of certain wonderfull over-flowings of Waters, now lately in Somersetshire, Norfolke, and other places of England'.

† Frances Wood, in *Somerset Memories and Traditions*, leaves us with a thumbnail sketch of the females who presided over these cumbrous contraptions—'The old ones, stout, and looking like gamps, always wore big sun-bonnets, and the young ones somehow always looked like seals. One never saw a pretty one.'

The areas economy is grounded firmly upon local manufacturing industries, agriculture and tourism. Fishing on a commercial basis has declined, but in the waters around Weston-super-Mare it is still possible to catch soles, shrimps, plaice, herring, sprats, conger eels, cod and salmon.*
Among leisure activities, sailing is popular—even though fast currents render the Channel dangerous for inexperienced—and there are well established yacht clubs at Burnham, Weston-super-Mare, Clevedon and Portishead.

Finally there is the holiday trade, and, in this particular department, the region does surprisingly well. Although the coastline lacks the hacked and fractured impressiveness of Cornwall or Pembrokeshire, the resorts have a demode charm of their own, and although the Channel waters are often described as lead-coloured and scummy, there is also a belief that because of this unsightly mud, the air had been inbued with medicinal qualities—so that, when the westerly breezes skim the ozone off the flats and sweep inland, sufferers from catarrh and allied ailments should deeply inhale the benefit.

---

* Larger creatures have, however, been recorded. In 1882, for instance, a sea-serpent was identified in the Channel. Earlier sightings that year described it as black, about 200 feet long, moving with corkscrew-like motions at approximately 25 miles per hour and leaving a greasy wake behind it.

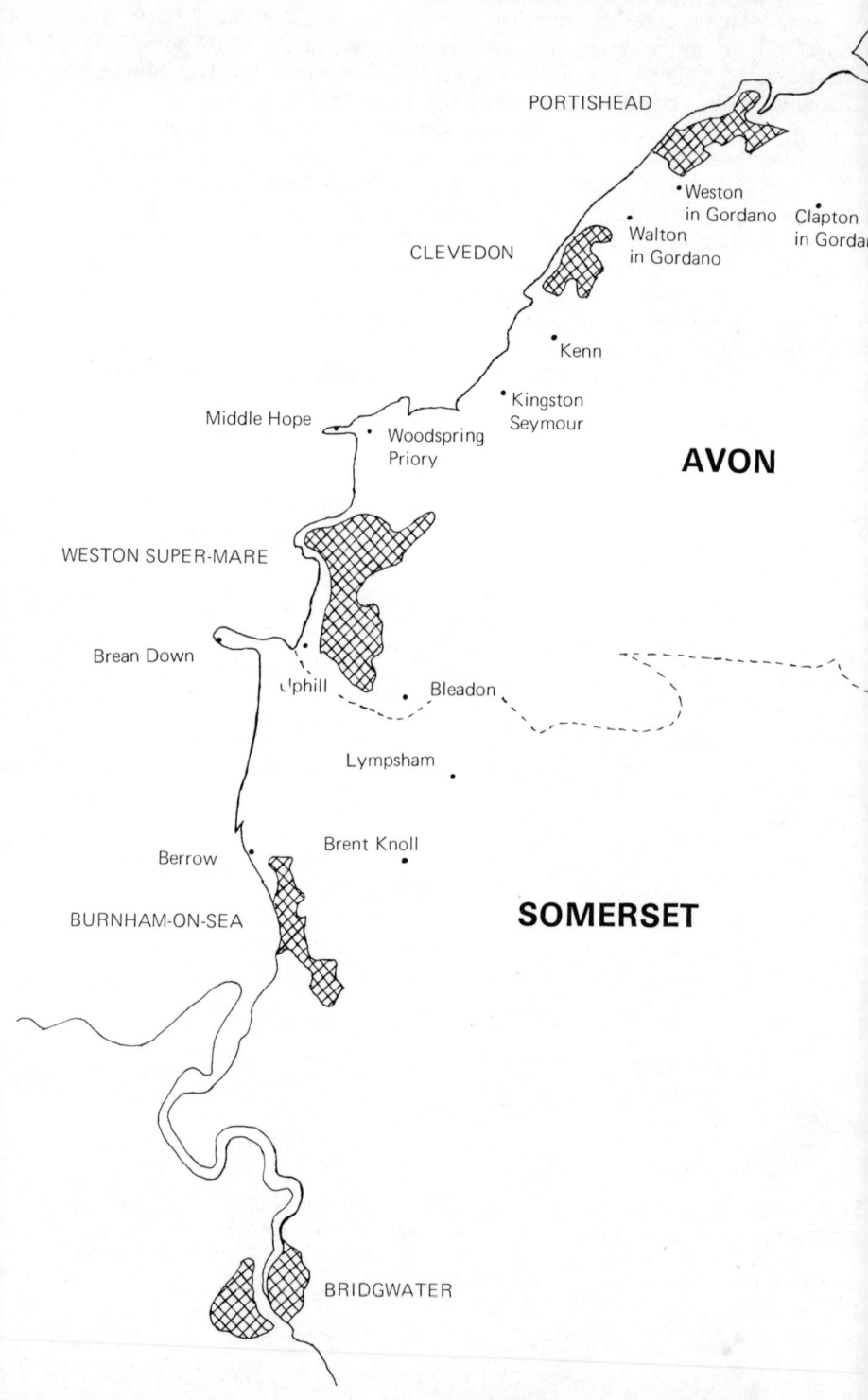

PORTISHEAD

FROM the Mariner's Path, Portishead first presents itself as rows of houses climbing a low wooded promontory, fringed by a butterscotch ribbon of sand, from which four huge chimneys protrude, like gigantic red cigars, or the spires of some futuristic cathedral designed by a maniac. Despite this, it is an agreeable place.

The Esplanade beach, admittedly, with its coarse gritty sand, manure-coloured reeds and contorted strata of red and brown rocks, is unremarkable, but the town has other blessings to count: woodland walks, a skilfully landscaped boating lake, good shops and ready access to Bristol.

Portishead's history—like that of Clevedon and Weston—is one of rapid expansion from the Regency Period onwards. Yet it has roots which delve deep into the soil of the past. According to Gerard's history of Somerset, the name derives from Port, a seafaring Saxon who visited these shores at the close of the eighth century A.D. The towns, Portland and Portbury, also celebrate this stalwart rover. This connection, tenuous although it may seem, has stuck and Portishead, or Porta's head or harbour, is the usual connotation.

It has been claimed by some archaeologists that the Wansdyke ends in Portishead. This immense rampart is believed to have been constructed by the Britons in their battles against the Anglo-Saxons around A.D. 770 and the remnants of the ancient camp crowning the Knoll are said to mark its western boundary. Recent evidence, however, tends to run counter to this theory.

The old town was centred round the Mill. Kipling's lines from Puck of Pook's Hill could have been aptly applied to this ancient foundation:

> See you that little mill that clacks,
> So busy by the brook?

> She has ground her corn and paid her tax
> Ever since the Domesday Book.

Collinson refers to it briefly in his eighteenth-century survey. 'A spring called Welly-Spring rises on Welly Hill about a mile from the church, and running in a small brook through the village falls thence into the main channel at the water-mill.' But in 1815, at the time of the Portbury drainage scheme, the mill was dismantled. Apparently its owner, by taking advantage of the high tides and allowing saltwater to collect behind his dam, was sabotaging much good reclamation work. Today only the Millstone remains, sunk into the wall outside the White Lion, like a primitive sunwheel symbol.

The town's maritime history is crammed with incident. Towards the end of the eighteenth century, Collinson noted that there were a number of market boats, carrying corn, cider, fish and other goods daily to Bristol and returning with bricks, tiles and timber. Beyond Woodhill Ridge is the traditional anchorage of Kingroad. This was the stopping-place for large numbers of vessels awaiting the right wind or tide to carry them downstream or inland to Bristol. Leland, in the sixteenth century, refers to it as Kyng's Rode and it has a history fraught with murder, smuggling, pirateering and other spirited activities. Frances Brett Young, in his poem about John Cabote, recalls the journey down this waterway:

> Over Avon's oozy bed
> We drifted seaward mile on mile
> Till we cleared the bluffs of Portishead
> And weathered Lundy Isle;

The development of steam power, however, robbed it of all its importance. Only the *Formidable*, an eighty-four-gun man-of-war adapted as a cadet-training ship, remained moored there until the foundation of the Nautical School in 1906 made it redundant. Steam packets also plied their trade at Portishead, notably the *Eagle*, the *Cambria* and the *Saint David*, dropping their passengers at the Parish Wharf or the Royal Hotel, depending on whether the tide was high or low.

* * *

Woodhill Bay, where most of the amenities for visitors are concentrated, is the strongest tourist magnet in the town. The Boating-lake occupies a central position. This elegant sheet of water—formerly a stagnant stretch of rhynes and withy beds called 'Rodmoor'—was dug out by the unemployed of Bristol. Tiny wooded islets stud its glassy-dark expanse, across which swans imperiously glide, demanding portions of any packed lunch in view.

The bay terminates in Battery Point—a smooth green promontory warted by a small lighthouse and warning-bell. Huddling beneath its grassy slopes, the vivid rectangle of the swimming pool gleams. Now unoccupied, the fort—though consistently manned—witnessed little heroism or bloodshed. During the Civil War, it served as a Royalist stronghold. The locals who occupied it, however, were not desirous of distinguishing themselves as tiger-hearted warriors. When they heard that a fighting force, headed by the victorious Sir Thomas Fairfax, intended to besiege them, they were greatly 'perplexed' by these tidings. Some of them were so offended and upset that they left immediately and went home. The others, after some dithering and procrastination, hastily forwarded the terms of an immediate surrender which was duly accepted on Wednesday, August 27th, 1645.

This was by no means the last incident in the life of the Battery. On August 25th, 1685, it was graced with the presence of James II and Prince George of Denmark. It was the occasion of the former's 'Western Tour', and, along with other noblemen, he inspected the troops. Subsequently it fell into a period of disuse, then, at the time of the Napoleonic threat, was garrisoned again. Finally it was used for submarine defence during the last two World Wars. Today, thanks to the efforts of the local council, no trace of it remains, but, in its place, are excellent views of the maritime traffic and the Welsh coast.

Denny Island is clearly identifiable from the Point. For such fragments of information as are extant concerning this sea-girt hillock, we are indebted to a certain Bristol journalist, who, pathetically anxious for a story, spent a night on its cheerless confines. He reported that the island was infested with rats that fed on seagulls that fed on rats. Mallow, tree mallow a large and hardy plant, is also reputed to grow there. Otherwise, like Rockall, there is damn all.

* * *

An even more insignificant uplift, Dungball Island, bars the mouth of the Avon. At the time when the Kingroad was flourishing, this was the stage on which was played the final act of may a grimy little drama. Sailors, found guilty of robbery, desertion and piracy, were sometimes gibbetted here, and there was also an unusual case of fratricide in the nineteenth century.

When Captain Samuel Goodere, R.N., decided that, were it not for the presence of his brother, Sir John Dinely Goodere, Bart., his private income would be augmented considerably, he formulated a plan to remove this obstacle to his prosperity.

A gang of ruffians from his crew were enlisted. There were ordered to kidnap Sir John and bring him back to Samuel Goodere's ship, the H.M.S. *Ruby*. The orders were carried out faithfully and, once on board, the worthy gentleman was strangled and his body disposed of.

Dungball Island was to form the climax of this incident. The murder was speedily detected and the conspirators traced. Captain Goodere was executed in Bristol in 1741. The actual murderers, bound and guarded, were ferried to Dungball. There they—in full view of all the busy traffic of the Kingroad—were hung in chains until the final jerkings of their bodies ceased.

In case anyone is hoping to explore this island today, it should be made clear that it no longer exists, and only a fiendish mind and several tons of gelignite could bring it into being again—it is incorporated into the main wall of Avonmouth Docks.

* * *

Beyond the Point is Woodlands Road which leads to the Royal Hotel. This building, in the neo-Tudor style, was built in 1830 at the time when

Portishead was beginning to expand. It is rather austere fabric, slate-coloured, angular, with near square-hooded windows and black bargeboard gables. When it was first built, it was highly thought of and held out as a perfect mingling of aestheticism and function. Mr Peter Brush, the artist, enthused over its conventional and modest virtues in a characteristically unrestrained manner—'Who can speak too oft, or too partially, of the modern-built hotel—a structure, planned by the late Mr Desmond, architect, Bristol; blending a correct Elizabethan taste, with the most perfect attention to convenience and comforts: and surrounded by beautiful scenery; shady walks, and "valleys green"—forming altogether, a delightful retreat from sense and folly . . .'

Around this part of Portishead, one is almost uneasily conscious of the immense sky-stabbing monoliths of the power station. The soaring red-brick spires of its chimney stacks could have inspired poetry from Blake. They are extraordinarily impressive and, set against the tangled and varicosed trees of the Knoll, make a powerful design. In actual fact, there are four stacks in all, two of them belonging to 'Station A' and the other pair to 'Station B'. The former establishment, coal-fired, was commissioned in 1929; its present output capacity is 96 megawatts from two turbo-alternators. The latter, 'Station B', runs on both coal and oil and has an output of 373 megawatts from six turbo-alternators. Noticeable, too, on the east side of the dock, are a slimmer pair of smouldering obelisks. These delicate spires represent the aspirations of Messrs Albright and Wilson.

*   *   *

The dock, which belongs to the Corporation of Bristol, was opened in 1879 and its chief coastwise imports are coal and oil for the electricity station, the latter being also pumped from offshore. Foreign imports include rock phosphate and timber. The depth of the water on the sill at the ordinary spring tide is 33 feet and in the dock 27 feet. Cargoes bound for the South Wales coal ports can lock out of Portishead and into Newport, Cardiff and Barry on the same tide.

The complex is, of course, built over the original 'pill' or tidal creek. No longer is it possible to reconstruct the topography of this tiny estuary. When it was adapted as a harbour for ocean-going vessels, the whole morphology of the spot was altered. The inlet was widened. Dredgers were brought in. The banks were fortified with walling. A lock was installed. Rail communications were fixed. As a result, Portishead lost its status as a local trading concern and became an element in a larger design.

Comprising three berths—Wharves 1, 2 and 3, the south side of the dock, to cater for the increase in Scandinavian imports, is now a specialised wood-pulp terminal with its own labour force. Some 87,000 tons were handled in the twelve months ending in September, 1973. South Wharf 1 is backed by an area of six acres on which stand six sheds for storage purposes. Wharf 2, six hundred feet in length, is fitted with an oil berth. Both are rail-connected. Wharf 3 is used primarily by Messrs Albright and Wilson, the chemical firm, and has special apparatus—Chiksan hydraulic marine arms—for handling

Portishead   The training ship *Formidable*—an 84-gun warship—remained moored at Portishead from 1869 to 1906

liquid phosphorus. Conveyor bands transport it to the factory. On the north side, the berths are for the preferential use of the Central Electricity Generating Board. Coal and oil are transferred to the adjoining power station.

Not far from dock is the White Lion. Formerly this was the old mill, and flour which was ground here would be loaded onto small trading crafts standing nearby. The mill, harnessing both the tide and the small stream which meandered across the Gordano Valley, was a focal point in the village. Hatches controlled the quantity of water released, and the millstone—comprising 17 tightly packed stones in an iron hoop—was probably used as a driving wheel and not a grindstone. Locals would once dive off the archway of the White Lion, which marks the end of the old sea-wall. In the autumn of 1848, the bank gave way, inundating large areas of the village and reducing the cattle population.

*   *   *

At the end of the High Street, complete with thatched roof and transomed and mullioned windows, stands the Grange. This residence—'the chief and capitall messuage situate in Portishead'—was acquired in January 1619 from William Winter of Clapton and his wife, Mary. At the time, it was in the tenure of the Parsons family, who had lived there for over a century, and this led to false ecclesiastical associations being bandied about: the 'Old Parsonage' or the 'Parson's Pool', as it was sometimes referred to. The watery connotations of the latter name probably derive from the filled-in moat which once encircled the house. Eve Wigan identifies it, along with its 100-acre estate, as the ancient Manor of North Weston, which was once held by the Arthurs of Clapton. Later it was occupied by that scourge of bankrupts and unsuccessful gamblers, James Tanner, bailiff of the Bristol Corporation.

Nearby, in Church Road South, is the fifteenth-century Manor House. This mellow edifice, with red-brick angles, has a polygonal turret and stone mullioned windows with square hood-moulds. Constructed of pinkish stone, it has claims to be the finest old house standing in the town. The windows, typically Tudor, are small with flat arched heads and grouped in twos and threes. Notable, too, are the triangular niches at the corners—the last faint remnants of tracery. The turret is another beguiling feature, and it has been suggested that it was added by Edward Morgan in order to get a view of the ships sailing up the Kingroad. Rutter records that, in his time, the hall was used as a cider cellar and contained an antique mantlepiece of carved oak; and, at the south-east end, there was an approach to an old oak staircase leading to the upper storey.

Adjoining the Manor is the Parish Church. In the Perpendicular style, the tower has a pierced parapet with four pinnacles and rises solidly from its surrounds of soft grass and lichen-encrusted tombs. Drastic alterations took place here in 1880, and the interior of the building never quite recovered from the shock, but the vaults of the Mohuns and of Sir Edward Fust deserve a brief inspection. A list of incumbents from Thomas de Bradford in 1320 down to the present day is on display in the porch.

Some distance from the church and borrowing the name of its patron saint, is another of the town's most celebrated spots—Saint Mary's Well. There was a belief once rampant that the water from this spring could restore or improve failing eyesight, and, as late as June 1890, a correspondent of the local paper observed a youth carrying water for this purpose.

* * *

One of Portishead's most admired buildings is the Nautical School. Facing the sea on the Mariner's Path between Clevedon and Portishead, its broad regular outline commands attention. Dull, reddy-grey and sprawling, what the fabric suffers from most, curiously enough, is its lack of flamboyance: the Wren-ish lantern is too small and insignificant; the Palladian details are only weakly developed; the Ionic motifs are broken by rather fiddly stringcourses; the upper windows are far too close to the eaves and, viewed as a whole, the structure—though striking in a ponderous way—lacks vitality.

A footpath from the school's entrance leads down to the beach. There, standing on a low rocky bluff, is the Black Nore Lighthouse, a graceful Dalek-like erection, supported by white tubular piers and cross-ties. It stands on delicate crane's legs, serenely gazing at the sea, forming a pleasing composition with the Welsh hills and passing ships. On February 19th, 1949, the St Vincent, a Bristol craft, got stranded on the adjacent mudbank. A number of photographs recorded this event. Many of them have a faintly comic look—the strutting lighthouse and the low sleek form of the motor collier—as if the latter had glided in to engage the other in conversation.

From the light, the Mariner's Path twists in and out the bays of the coast, and, on a hilltop overlooking Walton Bay, passes the Signal Station, a plain white tower standing about 141 feet above sea level. It is specially equipped for signalling by morse light, and is linked by private telephone with the Haven Master's office at Avonmouth.

Similarly concerned with vigilance at sea, though in a much larger way, is the Wireless Receiving and Transmitting Station, overlooking Black Nore Cave. Tall masts, which flex like silver wands in gales, transmit signals from here to ships all over the world and are of vital importance to Britain's communication network.

* * *

For the purpose of the present study, any historical matter included is bound to be fragmentary, but before leaving Portishead, it is instructive to evoke the hamlet as it appeared in the 1840s, on the brink of its expansion and development; for, upon a certain weighty testimony, it was a spot with charms that exceeded those of its rivals. There is a document, obtainable from the Bristol Reference Library, outlining the beauties of Portishead at the time when it was just beginning to assume significance. Written by amateur artist and professional man of leisure, Mr Peter Brush, it is addressed 'Portishead on Severn' and is a waggish monologue extolling the charms of the 'faery village' in exaggerated and half-humorous rhetoric. Portishead, Mr Brush confides to his friend, Timothy Carmine, is far superior to Minehead and its deficient attractions; to Blue Anchor and its inadequate accommodation; to Burnham and its rampart of sand-hills; to Weston-super-Mare and its interminable expanse of dingy and aguish moorland; to Clevedon and its shade-less Bath-built houses, with its swarms of masons, bricklayers, carpenters, glaziers, painters and other operatives busily and noisily preparing for 'the season'. These sights, in his own words, grieviously upset him—'tomahawked' his taste, drew 'notes of discord' from his nerves, and converted his Bile into a fluid 'black as night'. And then, approaching Portishead, a marvellous feeling of peace assailed his spirit as he . . . looked down from a limb of the far-spreading Mendip Hills, upon this El Dorado of villages: with its diversified vicinity, of water: rock: wood: umbrageous lanes; and health-inspiring elevations; studded, irregularly, with neat and comfortable dwellings . . .

Mr Brush even finds it in him to praise the colour of the water at Portishead, which, under the right atmospheric circumstances, assumes a colouring 'as fit for the canvas, as the waters of the Cam; the Isis; or of old Father Thames'.

The letter, though entertaining, is rather a precious and verbose exercise: replete with apt quotations, Latin tags, literary and Homeric illusions, one hesitates to quote it in full; for Mr Brush's sentences unwind like monstrous serpents, multi-bracketed, ponderous, with qualifying clauses tangling and twisting among the subjects and predicates. Nevertheless, the document constitutes a valid impression of Portishead's appearance when it was poised between a fishing village, a pleasure spot, and an expanding maritime concern. Since then, it has grown fast—as a port and commercial centre rather than a holiday retreat—and to recall the unsoiled 'faery village' of 150 years back would make unreasonable demands on even a poet's imagination.

The motive force behind Portishead's expansion was, of course, the Bristol Corporation. Their interest in the hamlet was partly a traditional one. As early as 1616, by deed of Mr John Bradford, of Wiltshire, they had purchased the whole of the manor of North Weston for £950. On January 16th of the same year, for the trifling sum of £200, they acquired the Grange and a further 100 acres of land, and then, after three years had elapsed, Capenor Court for the more considerable price of £500.

What circumstances inspired these purchases? This is not a question to which there is a neat answer. Portishead, in the seventeenth century, had a certain strategic and navigational importance. A garrison had been established there and the Kingroad was of major significance as an anchorage. Possibly it was that last factor which prompted the Corporation's action. Bristolians sensed that, with the flowering of their merchant trade, it would be a wise investment to acquire land on the coastal periphery of their city boundaries.

Nevertheless, after the acquisition of these estates, they did not follow up their initiative with any definite scheme. The Civil War intervened, and the property gently lingered on in their possession for two hundred years.

A mild dispute did, however, occur in the eighteenth century. In 1705 an enquiry was held, the purpose of which was to clearly distinguish between the rights and holdings of the Bristol Corporation in Portishead, as opposed to those of the Cokes, the contemporary lords of the manor of Portbury. As a result of this tribunal, substantial areas, including Woodhill Bay, Sheepwash Bay and the Point, were designated as the Coke's, while the whole of North Weston, the manor which had been acquired from the Winters, was declared by the jurors to come under the sway of Bristol.

Portishead, at that period, was little more than a tiny agricultural and fishing community, the former occupying the valley on the south side of the hill. It was also a pilot station, owning a few fishing smacks; and sprats, herrings, flat fish and shrimps constituted the principal catch. Nets were staked out on the beach below the Royal Hotel until well into the nineteenth century until, in fact, they were declared a navigation hazard and had to be removed. An old watch house—the coastguard's residence—stood on the west side of the pill, and a lane at the back of Adelaide Terrace, connecting the Point with the Church, comprised the main thoroughfare into the village. Woodhill Bay was swamp then known as 'Rodmoor'. The tide flowed far up the tidal creek to the sea-wall, standing where the White Lion is today, and there was a wharf where small craft unloaded coal and bricks in exchange for flour and local dairy produce. The overshot mill was working, grinding corn, and no villas occupied the seafront. By 1810 the situation was much the same.

The Bristol Corporation, however, were stirring. They had already, by excavating the New Cut, diverted the Avon and built a huge floating harbour in the centre of the city, and were looking for other spots in which to unclench their petals.

Portishead, naturally, was their first choice. The manor of Portbury had changed hands since the eighteenth century. Now it was owned by the energetic Squire Gordon. This gentleman's claim to distinction is as the landlord who 'enclosed' large areas of the parish. From 1815 onwards, at considerable personal cost, he re-divided and re-allocated land at Portishead and Portbury. The City, previously, had recommended such a course of action to ensure that all holdings were exploited to their utmost agricultural advantage. This included the closure of the mill which had a vested interest in water and bogginess.

Bristol City Corporation entered into negotiations with the squire, and after appeasing him with a 15-acre estate on Portishead Down, acquired a further 30 acres and swiftly proceeded to buy-up more land and extend their territorial claims.

Slowly a programme of change was implemented. Upon the random and spontaneous architecture of the old village was imposed a more regular and geometric plan. New footpaths were laid. The Market Cross—a monument whose beauty equalled its obstructiveness—was shifted from its site of authority to the churchyard. A road was driven through the village green. Old placenames received another baptism. A landing-stage was erected north of the Point; also, a cottage for a boatman and, to replace the water mill, a windmill was set up by the 'Washingpool' on the Down. Yet despite these adjustments, the village retained its essential identity.

Between 1820 and 1830 the town's appearance underwent a more dramatic metamorphosis. Landscape gardening then began in earnest. Portishead, Bristol Corporation decided, was to provide a charming little playground for its more influential citizens. A sum of £20,000 was lavished in converting this rude fishing-village into an expanse of asphalted drives, tree-shaded walks and stately substantial homes for the financially well-endowed. Eastwood, the Royal Hotel, the classically styled Bath-House (The Saltings), and many of the tall Tudor–Elizabethan mansions sprinkling the Point sprang up during the period. The village had come a long way from that first stark entry in the Domesday Record:

> William de Moncels holds Portesheve of the Bishop. Aluric cild it in the time of king Edward and paid geld for 8 hides. There is land for 8 ploughs. In demesne are 6 hides and 2 ploughs with 1 serf, and there are 9 villeins and 4 bordars with 5 ploughs and 2 hides.
>
> There are 8 beasts and 10 swine and 60 she-goats.
>
> There is a mill paying 8 shillings and 20 acres of meadow and 100 acres of pasture. Underwood 12 furlongs long and 3 furlongs broad.
>
> It was and is worth 70 shillings.

CLEVEDON

LIKE a porous crumbling effigy of Alfred Lord Tennyson, Clevedon* still retains its Victorian identity—even as the new housing estates spawn around the lower half of the town. Many contemporary writers, setting down their impression of the retreat, adopt a tone of lukewarm enthusiasm; they refer to it as a mellow and self-effacing watering-place, quieter and less vulgar than Weston-super-Mare. Few sing it praises with anything resembling fervour, but, on the other hand, none have been moved to spiritedly abuse the spot. As for its inhabitants, C. G. Harper stated that they neither cared for literature, nor walked much or strolled on the sands (for there are none), and that nothing really mattered to them. This is how he summarised their activities:

> They sit upon the rocks waiting for the next mealtime and refusing (rightly) to support the miserable creatures, who, calling themselves 'pierrots', infest the front. In the exiguous public gardens old ladies of both sexes knit impossible and useless articles or pretend to read the newspapers and wonder why they ever came to the place.

Today, naturally, things have changed, yet, in a curious way, a number of Harper's amusing—but not necessarily perceptive—observations remain relevant. The pierrots have disappeared entirely, but the large percentage of retired people persist in the town, and this accounts for its relatively high death rate. Also, an air of conservatism, both political and cultural, pervades the resort, and a mild furore was whipped up among its populace when it was integrated in the new county of Avon.

Easily accessible from Bath, it was once a fashionable watering-place, and

---

* The point at which the clive, or cliff, drops to form a dun, or valley.

it was among the favourite retreats of the Count D'Orsay, dandy, portrait painter and swashbuckling successor to Beau Brummel, who, on the eve of a duel, remarked: 'We are not fairly matched. If I were to wound him in the face, it would not matter; but if he were to wound me, ce serait vraiment dommage!'*

As with hundreds of seaside resorts, Clevedon's most characteristic architectural style is the grey Victorian villa: robustly constructed of mountain limestone, tall, gloomy, high-ceilinged, they perch on the rocks of Hangstone Quarry and proliferate around the skirts of Dial Hill and Strawberry Hill. Although many share basic similarities in design, the mode of decoration varies, and the fancy dress styles of the Revival Period adorn the facades of numerous residences: Burstead House, on Hill Road, for example, with its curved Dutch gables, is an attractive example of mock-Elizabethan work; Elton Road has buildings which nicely absorb the Italian influence, while bastard Gothic motifs recur everywhere with unfaltering monotony.

A string of Regency to mid-Victorian houses occupy Pier Beach. In peach, peppermint, white, pink and lemon, seen from a distance they have a gay, powdery, whitewashed look—like so many cubes of coloured chalk. Names such as Brunswick and Clarence houses commemorate the toppled dignitaries of a bygone age, while Waterloo House nostalgically harks back to the fields of Belgium.

Yet undoubtedly the most striking feature of the seafront is the 840 feet long pier. This graceful structure, with its famous gap and wispy silver pagoda, was completed in 1869†—but at the cost of at least one life:

> Yesterday afternoon, about half past four, a labourer, named Henry Groves, met his death in a frightful manner. In the construction of these works an iron boat is used to convey the men to and from a barge and portions of the work at high water. The boat has from the first been an unfortunate expense to the contractors by getting adrift etc.; it was therefore thought advisable to hoist it under the Pier—and yesterday afternoon, at the time mentioned, a gang of men was engaged in this duty. A windlass, or crab, was used in the work, and deceased had hold of a portion of rope known as the 'slack'. By some means the machinery of the crab slipped, and the drum rushed in, drawing the poor fellow round its narrow circumference, completely crushing him to death. (Clevedon Mercury, March 21st, 1868.)

On October 16th, 1970, the central section of the pier collapsed while it was being weight-tested, islanding the pavilion and landing-stage. This incident made international news and sparked off a local controversy as whether to demolish or restore the remaining structure.

What is striking about the pier is, that, unlike many other engineering accomplishments of the period, iron is used with economy and grace. Instead of

---

* See Max Beerbohm's essay, Dandies and Dandies.

† The event was considered sufficiently important to merit a woodcut in the Illustrated London News.

the arches being obscured by a dense network of criss-crossing ties and vertical supports, the outline is as clear and delicate as a Japanese etching. The fragile tin-hat of the pavilion is a good focal point, too, but the clutter of nissen huts and outbuildings distracts from its fine proportions.

The Pier Toll House, which has been compared to a sham castle resembling one of those chalk ornaments affixed to cakes, was designed by Mr Hans Price of Weston-super-Mare. Adjoining it, the Royal Pier Hotel, typical of the later Victorian period with its high-pitched roof and dormer windows, dates from 1868. Formerly it was called the Rock House Hotel, after the earlier Regency building which stood here for some time.

Further uphill, turning to the right, is Saint Antony's School, one of the town's classier buildings. In the neo-Greek style, with tapering window frames, it has a pedimented entrance with two Ionic columns. Next door is Whitsom House, a similar Regency structure, with a pretty mermaid moulded in plaster above the doorway. Both houses date from around 1825.

Ascending Marine Hill one enters Hill Road, the principal shopping centre for the upper half of the town. At the far end of this thoroughfare, adjoining the Gothic-Revivalist Congregational Church, is Burstead House. With its fancy gables, cresting and grainy yellow stonework this is a pretty piece of pseudo-Jacobean imitation. Recently, the Secretary of State has listed this building as one of the four properties in the area of special architectural and historic interest, the others being Birnbeck Pier, Birnbeck Pier Toll House and the Grand Pier at Weston.

Carrying further along Hill Road, we pass Christ Church and descend into Church Hill. On the left is the Bristol Hotel, on the right a tidy Regency block of tenements, their projecting eaves ascending the slope in a succession of abrupt arcs.

At the bottom of the hill is the Triangle. This junction of the Clevedon–Yatton and Clevedon–Bristol roads is marked by a tall red-tiled Clocktower, decorated in Elton Ware with the figure of Father Time. In January, 1926, the Rt. Hon. Lloyd George addressed a 'large and enthusiastic' open-air meeting here. He spoke with 'marked distinctness,' the awestruck populace hanging on to every word which issued from his whiskered lips.

* * *

The most commandingly situated church in Clevedon is Christchurch. It stands, stark and authoritarian, at the upper end of Highdale Road, with its four-pronged tower skewering the upper air. In the Early English style, it has the distinction of being attended regularly by Nurse Edith Cavell. This 'great daughter of a great nation' was a schoolgirl at Clevedon and was confirmed at the parish church in 1884.

Descending the hill, one first notices Highdale Court, with its delicate veranda and classic proportions: neat square windows at the top contrasting with the taller frames and fitted doors below.

Its neighbouring dwelling, the Council House—now the Woodspring

Housing Department—represents one of the more bearable incursions into Gothicism. It is, in fact, one of those not-very-inspiring slathers of borrowed details: crenellations, cusped bay windows and tiny ornamental pinnacles on the gables. Built of Cotswold stone, it was once occupied by the influential Braikenridge family of Brislington, Bristol, who bore the greater part of the cost of the nearby Christchurch.

Still further down, tree-shrouded and faintly eerie, is the entrance to Mount Elton. Many early guidebooks draw attention to this house as being something of a showpiece. With its carved bargeboards, pepperpot motifs and profusion of chimney-shafts, it does try harder than many other mock-Tudor facades to look its part. A wooden footbridge rather imperiously connects it with its grounds, which are separated by a high cutting carrying the roadway.

At the junction of Highdale Road and Old Street, one's eye is drawn to the small East Clevedon Post Office, and, still further along, the octopuscular complex of Hales' cake factory.

To the left, low, sturdy and conspicuous in shocking pink, is the Old Inn. Over a century ago, this was regarded as a sort of poor man's haven of rest, a place to relinquish mud-splashed capes and corroded boots—'In the winter, the ruddy log fire in the tap-room tempts the shivering wayfarer to enter, whilst in the heat of summer the tired excursionist is glad to quaff a cool tankard in the quiet shady parlour, the bow window of which overlooks the road.'

Walton Road penetrates the Swiss Valley, one of the more idyllic spots in the area. With its striking crucifix and All Saints' Church overshadowed by the Court Woods, the setting would pass muster in one of those low-budget Dracula movies. The woods, in fact, provide some of the best rambles in the area. Most of the tracks lead up to the Warren, a beautiful stretch of open heath overlooking the Tickenham and Gordano valleys.

By the wayside, on the right side of the road, is the finely-situated Crucifix. This potent religious symbol recalls the Alpine valleys of Germany or Switzerland. The figure of Christ, emaciated after the stylised manner, is deftly executed and has a haunting waif-like fragility.

On the east side of the valley, the spire of All Saints' emerges from the bristling jungle of foliage which clothes the hillside. Erected in 1860 at the cost of Rhoda, Lady Elton, the interior is elaborately-decorated with rose-windows in the transepts and marble-faced walls in the sanctuary. In 1887, under the new act, the first non-conformist funeral service was conducted here, the Rev. John Victor, of Copse Road Chapel, officiating. The church doors were bolted, two policemen stood on guard, but these precautions did not stop the vituperous Vicar of All Saints' from stating his feelings plainly. He attached a notice to the porch gate—'This church is closed by my orders during the perpetration of an act of sacrilege under the new Burial Act.'

The Tickenham Road is equally interesting. It skirts that residence fitting for a 'Prince of Hermits', Clevedon Court, and skates past the new motorway to Nailsea and Wraxall. A track forking off the highway leads up to Cadbury Camp. This earthwork, like the plain-an-gwaries of Cornwall, dates from the Iron Age and is an atmospheric and brooding spot: a green saucer-shaped enclosure rounded by low turfy ramparts. It is listed, in a recent book on the subject, among the haunted places of the British Isles.

* * *

A favourite spot in Clevedon in the summer is the Green Beach: a sheltered cove situated below the Victorian bandstand. This was built in 1887 and is used by visiting bands during the season. The panels encircling the tiled roof are decorated appropriately with harps, trumpets and sunflowers.

Before this structure was erected, a newsman wrote, the bands had a very hard time of it. Rampaging gales assaulted both the audiences and the musicians in a strictly impartial manner, scattering and dispersing their melodious strains like thistledown. The stand was put up in the way of being a 'humane appliance'.

The roadside nearby is decorated with a rather fancy drinking fountain. In actual fact, there are two such stylish oases in Clevedon, one conventional Gothic, the other modish Art Nouveau. The first of these, a stubby pinnacle, erected by the Rev. J. S. Neumann in memory of his deceased wife, Annie, is near the bandstand, while its companion, a more adventurous Rococo piece, decorated with blue, green, yellow and grey Doulton Ware, is built into the wall of the Pier Copse. A shell canopy enshrines the dribbling tap and the chipped and ruptured stonework. But it must have looked very pretty indeed on that day in 1895 when it was opened for the first time and a crowd of people queued to partake of its crystal liquid.

Church Hill, rising darkly above the swimming pool and boating-lake, can be clearly seen from the promenade running alongside the Green Beach. In April, thick masses of blackthorn blossom on its shaggy slopes, like shimmering wads of foam.

To the left as one continues along the promenade, it is possible to catch a glimpse of a high wall running the length of Elton Road. If one surmounts this defensive barrier, a view is gained of an expanse of playing fields, tennis courts, woodlands and a swimming pool This is the domain, strictly speaking, of St Brandon's, a girls' public school originally designed for daughters of clergymen. Gaunt and Colditz-like, the edifice is typically heavy nineteenth-century Elizabethan and has an imposing central turret. Any hearty male contemplating forcing an entry into this glade of gym-slipped sylphs and hockey-playing woodnymphs must first be prepared to serenade a pack of snarling Alsatians.

A trim mustard-coloured Regency building is visible admidst the trees and shrubbery of Church Hill. Known as the Salthouse Hotel, this pub and restaurant is a favourite entertainment spot in summer: cabaret, apart from the antics of the clientele, includes pop groups, comedians and various solo spots. In the eighteenth century, two primitive cottages are said to have stood here, the occupants of which, being very poor, could not afford salt; so, instead of buying it, they built pools confining the inflowing tide; by evaporation, they retrieved the saline deposit. Hence the name.

Church Hill's neighbouring height, Wain's Hill, has the remains of Napoleonic military installations on its summit and an Iron Age Camp, the embankments of which, in various places, rise to a height of four feet and follow the contours of the hill.

In a hollow between these two grassy eminences, the parish church of Saint Andrew nestles contentedly, like an old grey rabbit at crop. In the Norman and Perpendicular styles, and dating originally from the eleventh century, the building contains a tablet to Arthur Hallam (Tennyson's much-mourned friend) and an incised effigy of Sir Thomas Clevedon, a knight whose family inherited the Manor after the Norman Conquest.

The recumbent figure of a child, with folded hands, standing opposite the pulpit, represents Phillipa Ethelreda, the little daughter of the Wake* family,

Clevedon   St Andrew's Church

who died in 1633 aged seven years. The Wakes were descended from the de Clevedon family and held the Manor for eight generations.

The central embattled tower contains a peal of bells and the old tenor-bell bears the following inscription:

> I to the Church the living call
> And to the grave do summon all. 1725.

*   *   *

Of all Clevedon's buildings, the most venerated showpiece is Clevedon Court. This has been described by Buckley as 'unquestionably the most valuable relic of Early Domestic architecture in England.' Dating from the reign of Edward II, it was restored in the Tudor period and has since recieved

* The Wake's family motto, 'Vigilate et orate' (Wake or watch and pray), through the efforts of the late Mrs R. G. Burden, is now incorporated in the town's coat of arms.

15

many additions and alterations. The Manor has numerous original features: a fourteenth-century chapel, a terraced garden, a well-stocked library and portrait gallery, a collection of Nailsea glass and china, a collection of watercolour paintings and other illustrations depicting the history of the Great Western Railway, and a great hall retaining the oak panelling and carved chimney-piece of the Tudor period.

The Eltons, who have occupied the Manor from 1709, are Clevedon's most consequential landlords. Originally from Herefordshire, they had already strongly established themselves as prosperous Bristol merchants before they purchased the Court. Rapidly negotiating social hurdles, Abraham Elton was to graduate from Sheriff to Mayor of Bristol. By 1717 he was a Baronet, and from 1722 until his death in 1728 he represented Bristol as Member of Parliament. The conferring of the title, in particular, provoked some unwarranted gibes as to his original background:

> In days of yore, old Abraham Elt,
> When living, had nor sword nor belt.
> But now his son, Sir Abraham Elton,
> Being knighted, hath both sword and belt on.

The late Baronet, Sir Edmund Elton, invented a vividly-coloured pottery called Elton Ware, the properties of which were summarised by Professor Church in language that combines vigour with vagueness—'It has achieved a decided and general success by virtue of the thorough soundness and extreme hardness of its fabric, the freshness and temperance of its forms, the appropriateness of its decoration and the rich quality of its colour.' The Triangle Clock, which he presented to the town in honour of Queen Victoria's Diamond Jubilee, is decorated with examples of this brilliant crackle-glazed substance. The secret process by which it was manufactured died with him.

Although little is known about the early history of Clevedon, documents relating to the various incumbents of the manor survive. An outline history would run along the following lines. At the time of Edward the Confessor it was owned by John the Dane, and, after the conquest, it fell into the hands of Matthew de Moretaine, the antecedents of whom—taking their inspiration from the locality—are said to have assumed the name of Clevedon. Sir John de Clevedon, who died in 1336, is thought to have built the Court around 1320. His son, Edmund, died leaving no male heir, and the holding passed by marriage to Edmund Hogshaw, and thence to his sister's spouse, John Bluet. The next owner was Sir Thomas Lovell, the daughter of whom married Sir Thomas Wake who died in 1459. The Wake's line, nevertheless, presided over the estate until Charles II's reign. Then, in 1630, Sir Baldwin Wake sold the manor to John Digby, first Earl of Bristol. The property, on the death of the third Earl, was acquired by Sir Abraham Elton in 1709.

When Abraham Elton moved into his new home, Clevedon was made up of the church, rectory and clusters of farmers' and fishermen's dwellings. And it was to continue that way for another hundred years, until, in fact, the advent of the nineteenth century.

Even then the first decade saw little progress, but, after another had drifted by, work was undertaken with zeal and determination. Mr Hollyman, the proprietor of the Old Inn, was one of the town's first developers, being responsible for the construction of the Rock House Hotel (Royal Pier) about 1822. Four years later, the Bristol Inn was built, with good stabling facilities for both animals and humans. At that time also, the Royal Hotel (Franciscan Friary) was under construction, to later become overrun by sandalled feet, tonsured heads and chanting voices. Then, from 1820 to 1830, some of Clevedon's finest houses materialised: the pedimented neo-Greek villas of Wellington Terrace, the finely-proportioned flats of upper Highdale Road, the pleasing—though architecturally humdrum—row of boarding-houses lining the seafront, and the balconied residences situated above the ridge of Hill Road.

From about 1835 or so, the architectural trend began to move away from the Classical and Grecian, to the sombre, brooding and Gothic. And so, within Clevedon, the character of building changed, and, for the next seventy years, they spread unchecked, thousands of drably imposing facades, some with embattled bay-windows, some with irrelevant trefoil patterning, some with bargeboard gables, strapwork decoration and glowering gargoyles

Clevedon   The pier soon after its collapse in October 1970

above the entrances. Elton Road, for example, with its massive four-square Victorian–Classical hybrids (Norfolk and Anglesey House), was opened in 1855, and Linden Road (one of the few thoroughfares with happy examples of Elizabethan borrowings) dates from 1857.

Ironically, all this swift, smothering development was to drastically alter the town's appearance and relevance. What was once a place to be looked-at and admired became a place to be built-on and lived-in, and, as fast as the new buildings were erected, the landscape which had endeared the hamlet to the early tourist disappeared from sight.

Now the land surface of the town has been almost totally concealed. This statement can be confirmed by comparing the town today with any early nineteenth-century print. A glance will reveal the nature of the transition: small hills were flattened, limestone crags were screened by villas, treeclad slopes were asphalted and converted into roads, and it is now almost impossible to recognise the fact that Clevedon was once held to be the centre of a scenically spectacular little area, a miniature karst region of frost-gnawed crags and tree-studded ravines. Some of these topographical features are, of course, still available for viewing today, but their appeal is now minimal. Easy access and the general tidying-up process that accompanies development has gelded what wildness they once possessed.

Another decisive factor was scale. When the high Victorian villas were built, they dwarfed the tiny twisting paths and ravines. The houses, for example, fronting the zigzag path leading down to Hill Road, conceal what was formerly a magnificent upsweep of downland and rock, rising a clear three hundred feet from the shores of the Severn. From Wellington Terrace, in 1830, it was possible to gain an unbroken panorama of the bay, with fertile fields, interspersed with copses, extending to the sea, and of the parish church, tight in its green cleft, as plumes of spray exploded like rockets against the cliffs below.

But—and this is true of Portishead and Weston—over-zealous building has now masked these views, and Clevedon, like Bath or Bristol, has increasingly become a town of walks between walls. But this should not necessarily imply criticism, for, finally, people must have homes, and it must be conceded that, had our forefathers nurtured scruples, to the point of daintily refraining from building in a valley or on a hilltop because it looked pretty, it is doubtful whether any descendants would have survived to criticise their patterns of settlement.

Besides, it has become hackneyed to regard the development of a town's amenities and natural resources as synonymous with despoilation. A correspondent to the 'Mercury', of April 6th, 1867, wrote—'Nearly 20 years ago, when I first came to Clevedon by coach, the village did look inviting, but now, ugh, you have ruined it. What with the Local Board, or Local Humbug, and trumpery railway, gas lights, reservoirs of water and one thing and another, why, 'tis not safe to live here. And a pier, whoever heard anything so foolhardy—a pier at Clevedon—why, gad-a-massy, 'twill make the place ten times worse than it is.'

* * *

THE FRANCISCAN FRIARY

An order of Franciscan monks reside at Clevedon. They established themselves first in the town in 1882 after the French government passed an edict dissolving monastic institutions. Since then, they have lived here quietly, devoting their energies to the study of philosophy, canon law, and the fathers of the church. Modest and hardworking, they stroll about in rudimentary sandals and use large knotted cords to hold in their waists. Being highminded and fastidious souls, they do not welcome the attentions of matey vulgarians smirking at their haircuts, quizzing them what they are wearing under their habits, or telling them long and tedious jokes about crafty abbots and pulchritudinous nuns.

WALTON ST MARY'S
AND
THE GORDANO VALLEY

THE parish of Walton St Mary's is only a short walk from the seafront at Clevedon. Originally dating from the thirteenth century the church was rebuilt and reconsecrated in 1870. The oldest part remains the tower which dates from the fifteenth century. In the churchyard stands an ancient stone cross, about 20 feet in height, supported by three stone steps. The whole enclosure is now hemmed in by tall complacent villas, but its atmosphere was once sufficiently chilling to move Collinson to indulge in one of his more Gothic flights:

> The cemetry is surrounded by a stone wall, and is to this day the place of sepulchre of the poor of Walton parish, whose bones rest here quietly, for here the hallowed soil is but seldom trod even by the foot of the antiquarian; and the traveller who visits this solitary domain is welcomed by no other sounds than the howling of the winds, the roaring of the sea, the lowing of the cattle and the bleating of the sheep upon the neighbouring mountains.

If the word 'mountain' seems inappropriate considering that none of the nearby hills exceed 300 feet, it should be borne in mind that the historian was writing before extensive urban development had masked the landscape—a time when miniature ravines and pygmy crags could assume awesome proportions.

When the foundations for the new church were being dug out, a quantity of fossilized lead was discovered at the foot of the tower, together with a number of skeletons with damaged skulls. These were thought to have belonged to a band of Roundhead soldiers who set alight to the village of Stoke-super-Mare. This hamlet, of Royalist sympathies, was perched on the clifftops overlooking Ladye Bay and disappeared around 1600.

At the sight of Cromwell's troops, the men of the village evacuated their families and retreated to the tower of Saint Paul's Church. When the soldiers stormed this building, they stemmed their attack by pouring molten lead on them—or so the story goes. Anyhow, the village of Stoke was abandoned permanently, the inhabitants moving to the valley where Walton-in-Gordano is today. And, as for Saint Paul's Church, total dereliction overcame it until it was re-built and re-dedicated to Saint Mary. And that is why Walton has two parish churches.

Not far from the church, at the termination of Bay Road, are a steep flight of stone steps leading down to Ladye Bay. This precipitous cove, thickly plastered with vegetation and littered with great masses of dislodged rock, marks the line of a geological fault and is noted for its 'potato stones': compact shaley sandstones with crystal formations.

Along the cliffs, between the pier and the bay, are the Smuggler's Steps. These are said to have been constructed as bathing or paddling steps to serve the houses in Wellington Terrace, but it seems an exposed and perilous spot for such aimiable diversions and was probably erected as an exciting and precarious clifftop descent to gain a fine view of the Channel and the passing ships. Today, this staircase is muddy, slippery, incomplete and overgrown with ivy and moss. Its inaccessibility and bad state of repair renders it dangerous.

Just beyond Ladye Bay Point, formed by the dislocated rock strata, is Babyface Cave, so named because of the curious round head engraved on the stone beneath the entrance hatch. Most likely this was the work of someone with a cold chisel and hammer who had nothing else better to do, but there have been murmurings about it being a representation of the Celtic god, Bran. This, to say the least, is a very long shot.

On the hill above Ladye Bay is Walton Castle. This charming folly, erected in the reign of James I, is rapidly falling apart and energetic tourists are strongly discouraged from attempting to scale its tottering battlements. Yet, at one time, its cross-windows and octagonal centre provoked admiration. Sir Nikolaus Pevsner described it as 'a remarkable piece of ornamental planning'; the more grumpy C. G. Harper dismissed it as 'a flimsy and fast-decaying sham'. Certainly, in the 1790s, it was quite a substantial ruin:

> The building is of octangular form, having a round tower at each angle, and an embattled wall between each. In the centre of the area stands the keep or citadel, which is also octangular and has a small turret of the same shape on the south-east side; the roof and floors are fallen in, and no use made of any part of the castle except a small portion of the ballium which serves as a dairy for the tenant of the adjoining farm.

Of its history little can be said. Built around 1620 by the first Lord Poulett, an ancient earthwork was flattened to make way for its foundations. An early sketch of it shows it to have been a very elaborate and fancy hunting lodge indeed. Only the crumbling bones of a few angle towers and a shattered keep remains upright today. Silent, grey, softly melting to powder and loose stonework, it stands aloof, besieged by the sharp whizz of golf balls.

* * *

Running above Ladye Bay is the Mariners' Path. If followed to the end, it emerges at Portishead: a walk of about five miles winding between small bays and inlets and spasmodic eruptions of greenery. The footpath climbs up past the Signal Station and is lined by coppery bracken, yellow furze and blackberry bushes. The low rugged cliffs project in two distinct layers, indicating the line of an ancient beach, and they are speckled with quartz pebbles, like sultanas in a huge stodgy pudding.

A hundred or so years ago, it was common to find samphire gatherers on the rocks of this coast; and, in fact, Coleridge recorded their presence in one of his early notebooks. This estuarine plant, with its fleshy, succulent, salt-tasting stalks and leaves, was once much favoured both as a vegetable and a basis for sauce. The French call it the herb of Saint Peter; for like that stalwart disciple, it is founded on a rock. 'It is the pleasantest sauce, most familiar and best agreeing with man's body,' was the verdict of Gerard.

An indication of the esteem in which it was formerly held can be gauged by consulting the annals of Weston-super-Mare. A surgeon, it is recorded, accepted a peck of samphire by way of payment for setting a broken arm. Shakespeare was also aware of its nutritional value: Edgar, that remarkably fluent idiot, refers to it in the famous 'Dover Cliff' episode in 'King Lear'. Nor does its literary lineage end there. An equally vigorous dramatist, J. M. Synge, in 'The Playboy of the Western World', possibly had it in mind at the close of the action when his central character, Christy Mahon, remarks—'Cut the rope, Pegeen, and I'll quit the lot of you, and live from this out like the madmen of Keel, eating muck and green weeds off the face of the cliffs.'

In July and August, colonies of it flower on ledges and clifftops, displaying clusters of miniscule yellow buds with sticky-shiny surfaces. Identification never poses a problem. Its strong scalpel-like leaves and distinctive spicy odour cannot be mistaken.

For anyone wishing to put its culinary qualities to test, it should be borne in mind that samphire, like asparagus, is a succulent and should be boiled for about ten minutes in unsalted water and served with melted butter—or, if young and fresh, eaten direct as a vegetable in a salad. Pickling is another alternative.

*   *   *

Forking off to the right, approximately one and a half miles beyond Ladye Bay, is the route which leads down into the Gordano Valley. This secluded inlet, like the brush of a fox, tapers to a fine point at Clevedon; from the town itself, it roughly extends in a north-easterly direction for five miles. On each side rise wooded hill ridges composed of carboniferous limestone; the soil in the valley is peat overlain in parts by alluvial clay. This region, because of its varied bird and plant life, is protected in certain areas: Water Rail, Moorhen, Snipe, Lapwing and Grasshopper Warbler are common; also, in some of the quarry workings, Kestrels breed regularly. The southern side of the valley has large unworked deposits of coal, copper and lead.

A string of small villages occupy the vale. The nearest of these to the

Mariners' Path—Walton-in-Gordano—has a beguiling setting, with pink and grey stone cottages tumbled haphazardly among rocks and trees, and a tiny brook fringed with vivid ferns and cresses running down the hill, like a thread of melting grass, and past the Parish Church of Saint Paul. This stone building, in the Early English style, was built in 1839 and restored in 1874. The font belonged to the old church of Walton Saint Mary's. Its tiny thumb-stump of a tower makes a refreshing change from dagger-sharp pinnacles and phallic spires.

One building here, the Old Parsonage, may be of passing interest to criminologists, being leased for a number of years to Samuel Savile Kent, a Victorian factory inspector whose name flashed across the headlines, when, in June 1861, his three-year-old son was murdered at Road Hill House, Wiltshire. Was Kent guilty? The evidence emerged as complex, puzzling and contradictory, and—among specialists in this field—still excites argument and speculation. His relations with his wife while he was staying at Walton were far from ideal, and it was popularly rumoured that Mrs Kent's life was one of domestic enslavement. Yet Mr Weeks, the gardener, retained fond memories of Mr Kent, speaking of him as a 'kind master' and a friend to the poor. A relative was eventually convicted of the murder. The most recent study of this intrigue is 'Saint—with red hands' by Iseult Bridges.

* * *

Striking east, about one and a half miles along the B 3124, is the village of Weston-in-Gordano. The Parish Church of SS Peter and Paul, originally of the eleventh century, was rebuilt in the Perpendicular style about 1480.

In the churchyard, close to the wall, is a rather plain altar-tomb, believed to be that of Richard de Perceval, the crusader, on less than substantial evidence. Nowadays it is rather a commonplace sepulchre, but formerly it was a very showy and elaborate casket. Richly-inlaid with latten, crowned by a canopy upheld by six pillars—no village swineherd could have rested easy in it. Roundheads and other iconoclasts have, however, streamlined its contours.

It is of interest to note in passing that the north side of the churchyard was formerly called 'The Devil's Side', being the plot reserved for unbaptised infants, suicides, those who died without the benefit of the clergy, and other souls whose unworthiness merited special treatment.

Perceval is believed to have been a knight of uncommon valour. In the service of King Richard I, he entered Palestine in 1190. There is a story about him that, having lost his leg in armed combat, he soldiered on until another violent sortie left him bereft of an arm; but still, with his horse's bridle in his teeth, he continued to club and hack his assailants until, from severe arterial bleeding, he fell dead off his horse. This story, gory-fanciful as it is, probably has some foundation: the Perceval family crest depicts an armed knight, on horseback, with one leg severed.

The later Perceval history is also eventful. Thomas Perceval had the unenviable task of guiding the family fortunes through the Civil War; for being staunch Royalists, they were exposed to a number of indignities. According

Dock, Portishead,
rtant as a
-pulp terminal.

The Manor House, Church Road South, Portishead. Window detail in top right hand corner.

 Nautical School,
re Road,
rtishead.

Woodhill Road, Portishead. Interesting in that it marks the transition from the modest, regular and Classical, to the counterfeit pretensions of the Victorian era.

Power Station, Portishead, as seen from Woodlands Road.

Woodhill Road, Portishead.

The Beach,
Woodhill Bay,
Portishead.

The Millstone,
the White Lion,
Portishead.

Woodhill Bay,
Portishead.

The Grange,
High Street,
Portishead.

The Royal Hotel,
Woodlands Road,
Portishead.

The Lighthouse,
Battery Point,
Portishead.

Anthony's School, Marine Hill, Clevedon.

Ornament, Marine Hill, Clevedon.

untain, Alexandra Road, Clevedon.

Fountain, Elton Road, Clevedon.

St Mary's Church, Walton, Clevedon.

Stone Cross, St Mary's Church, Walton.

Ladye Bay, Walton, Clevedon.

Walton Castle, Walton, Clevedon.

er Toll House,
Clevedon.

Christ Church, Clevedon, from the corner of Linden Road.

Burstead House,
Hill Road, Clevedon.

The Council House,
Highdale Road,
Clevedon.

All Saints' Church, Swiss Valley, Clevedon.

Samphire, the Pill, Clevedon.

Crucifix, Swiss Valley, Clevedon.

to Collinson, Parliamentary forces ransacked the house, destroyed pertinent family documents and defaced the tombs of their ancestors.

Nevertheless, the family, being of the stuff their monuments are made, weathered the storm, and, at the time of the Restoration, were still in the Gordano Valley, living peaceably and prosperously. The following century, however, saw the dramatic dwindling of their influence, and, eventually, Anne Perceval, the last of the direct line, sold up the manor house and surrounding properties. The community's tap-roots were finally severed.

Yet, by some inexplicable alchemy of attraction, this tough and tenacious family was to re-establish its links with Gordano in the years 1910–11. Two sisters, Jane and Fanny Perceval, of Royal York Crescent, Clifton, contacted the vicar of Weston and told him of their resolution to erect two monuments in the church: a window to the memory of James, Richard and Ascelin Perceval, and a cross to their grandfather, the Honourable Spencer Perceval, the Prime Minister who was assassinated.

Uncanny psychic phenomena surrounds the latter incident. On a morning in 1812, Spencer Perceval related to his family an account of a disturbing dream he had experienced the previous night. He was walking through the lobby of the House of Commons—a distraught looking individual ran up to him brandishing a pistol and wearing a green jacket with shiny buttons—the gun exploded—all went black. From that last detail, the Prime Minister inferred that he had been shot dead. His family, shocked and upset, pleaded with him not to attend the House that morning. Waiving aside their concern, he declared important business could not be suspended on account of a mere dream. So he attended the Commons, as usual, and, while he was passing through the lobby, a man emerged from behind one of the pillars and shot him through the breast. The man, John Bellingham, a merchant who attributed his bankruptcy to government measures, was wearing a green coat with brass buttons.

More oddly still, Perceval was not the first man to be visited by this dream. John Williams, a gentleman of Redruth, Cornwall, had it a week before the event materialised. So vividly did it impress him that he considered travelling to London and warning the Prime Minister, but abandoned the idea. His ardour was dampened by the laughter and scepticism of his friends.

* * *

A dirt-track crosses the B 3124 at right angles and leads on to Weston Moor. Alkaline springs, issuing from the base of limestone ridges, collect in this basin and form genuine fenland: *Phragmites* reed with nesting colonies of sedge and reed warblers in the marshy patches, and plants such as ragged robin, yellow iris and marsh orchids in the grassland areas. The natural transition, via aquatic plants to alder, birch and willow carr, is constantly taking place and eliminating the watery stretches. Huge fly-ash rubbish tips—the gift of Portishead Power Station—squat on the eastern fringes of the moor. The valley bed comprises mainly post-glacial peat deposits striking to a depth of 15 feet; and Weston Moor has been designated a Nature Reserve; Weston Big Wood, a Site of Special Scientific Interest.

On the Clapton side of the valley, the sweeping aggressive flyovers of the M5 dominate the traditional farm buildings. They are not, however, the first signs of industry to mark this quiet spot. On the wooded hillside, near the Black Horse Inn, are derelict and overgrown pitheads. Lower down are mounds of slag. Coal was once worked here for upwards of a century—Collinson described in 1791 as quick-kindling and sulphurous.

As for the inn itself, its prominent signboard continues to attract many visitors from the surrounding countryside. Its decor remains bare and wooden, and this accounts for much of its popularity. Myrtle Cottage, standing adjacent, is an ancient structure despite its re-worked windows—possibly early seventeenth century? Pevsner, in his architectural survey of N. Somerset, mentions as noteworthy a cottage in Wood Lane; it has three-light mullioned windows and is dated 1766; also, between Prior's Wood and Caswell Cross, the Iron Age system of lynchets ascending the ridge.

The village of Clapton-in-Gordano proper is a dispersed settlement straggled along the 100-foot contour. In a field near here, a spectacular find of some 5000 Roman coins was made in 1924.

The church of Saint Michael, dating from about 1250, has a Perpendicular tower and a Norman tympanium. The building is not immediately noticeable from the Portbury road which skirts it, but, looking upwards, one is immediately struck by its presence. Like some gigantic armoured reptile, it grips a swelling pillow of turf and looms above the flatlands of the valley. The elevated setting—far above the marshes and reed-swamps—was once necessary for practical reasons, but today, with the coming of intense cultivation and effective drainage, it has a remote predatory air. On the same level as the church, running along the southern hill ridge, the gin-pink scar of the M5 cutting is prominent.

A manor house of the fourteenth century, Clapton Court faces the church. This edifice, solidly constructed of Triassic Sandstone, is a mere remnant of a once extensive building. Undoubtedly its most striking original feature is the square embattled tower. Entered through a broadly-moulded archway, it is of three storeys, the second of which has a fireplace and a corbelled staircase leading to the lookout at the top. The original plan of the manor, it has been suggested, was based upon a parallelogram, running east to west, the tower being sited to the north. The coat of arms of the Arthur family is carved above one of the fifteenth-century windows, and the same coat impaling Berkeley decorates the entrance.

In the buttery, the storeroom behind the baronial hall, was found an elaborate and richly-carved wooden screen, which, in the opinion of Mr J. H. Parker, is the most remarkable of its type in existence. It can now, on request, be viewed in the parish church.

The manor was the seat of the Arthur family. They, like the Percevals, were the lions of the Gordano Valley, powerful, rich and well-connected. They were not, however, above common litigation, for, in 1492, their name figured in a lawsuit. A certain John Payne claimed that John Arthur, heir to the manors of Weston and Ashcombe, had trespassed upon his fishing rights at 'Ankers Hed' and craftily skulked off with a hundred horseloads of 'barons' (sprats), four hundred 'tubbelyns' (young cod), three hundred 'haddockes' and two hundred 'whitynges'. John Arthur, not uningeniously, contested this claim, pointing out that the alleged poaching had taken place on land, which, on the ebbing tide, was left uncovered and therefore constituted part of the foreshore of which his father, John Arthur, happened to be the owner.

The Arthur family, with the passing of time, married into the Winters, who, in their turn, became lords of the manor. But they were far less prudent in the handling of their financial affairs, and Henry Winter, on his deathbed, was forced to relinquish the estates of Clapton and Weston-super-Mare.

In Saint Michael's Church are monuments to the Winter family, and they are oddly moving. There, in the purgatorial cold, Henry Winter, wastrel and gambler, kneels facing his wife, Katharine. Their prayers are for the soul of their dead child, Edmund, seated on a small thronelike chair, with a skull in his right hand. Death is there, too, in the form of heraldic symbols—an inverted torch, shorn grass and a closed book. The dedication runs—'Here lyeth the body of Edmund, son of Henry Winter Esq., who departed this life November 25th, Anno Domini 1672.'

The practice of cramming church interiors with miscellaneous statuary is a curious one and would seem to be based on Christian doubt as much as faith. However deeply religious, few contemplate with any certainty an after-life, and so, by way of providing a substitute presence, they prefer to leave something behind to vouchsafe that they once lived and breathed and moved. As these interior furnishings build up over the years, the church is transformed into a sort of funereal art gallery, a repository of tombs, tablets, marble figures, woodcarvings, commemorating sundry ecclesiastics, local philanthropists and business men—a mausoleum of exploded reputations. But, finally, what such monuments seem to express is a desire to stay on indefinitely, an unwillingness to be borne away to an unspecified destiny. They are a final desperate shriek of 'I was here!' before the personality topples into the gulf of oblivion.

Finally, it would be a pity to leave Clapton without first quoting a writer, who, with rich Keatsian rotundities of style, evokes the church and the manor house as they might have appeared to medieval eyes:

> One's first sight of the hamlet's little thirteenth-century building, dedicated to St. Michael and All Angels, is impressive in the extreme ... At its feet stretches the Gordano Valley, once a marsh and often, in past centuries, covered by the salt water of the Severn Sea. When, in former times, the floodwater lapped against the hill, the grey old church, standing gaunt and naked in the white light of the morning sky, must have presented a romantic picture ... Below the church and sheltered by its mound, is the old manor house of the Arthur family, formerly one of the county's grandest homes. Time was, centuries ago, when squires in armour, on the eve of the Crusades, climbed the steep hilltop from the house to lay their weapons on the altar, and to ask, in all night vigil, for the blessing of Mother Church ... Through the waving grass went pages with falcons on their wrists, hunting the game that sheltered in the impenetratable Clapton

Woods. In the Great Park behind the Manor House—now all but obliterated—genteel dames sat in their arbours, listening to the songs of troubadours, or watching their menfolk engaging in the lists for the garlands of some lovely lady ... Little now remains of the magic of the past, but sometimes, in the dusk of evening, when the lighted windows of the church reflect the gleam of candles, and the singing of the little congregation comes down the hill, across the valley, one may be tempted to imagine that the 'great days' have come back once more ...

It would be pleasant to indulge Frederick Jones further. Cutting him off, one feels, is rather like putting a bullet through the breast of a lark in midflight.

* * *

The parish of Easton-in-Gordano, or Saint George's, is the nearest of the four to Bristol. Once it was surrounded almost entirely by water. The parish church, dedicated to Saint George, was rebuilt in 1872 and has a register dating from 1559. The tower, however, is medieval with four pinnacles, buttresses and battlements. In the graveyard are a number of interesting epitaphs, one of which for its tersity is worth quoting:

> In love he liv'd in water he died
> Life was desired but God denied.

This, despite its compact pithiness, is not so interesting as the one at Clapton, relating the misfortunes of a young sailor:

> Both stout and strong was I
> In Plymouth Hospital to die
> I did escape the raging seas
> And so at Plymouth end my days
> At nineteen years my doom I met
> Strange the sun in the morning set
> Sudden the small pox seized me
> And terminated all my misery.

Yet, for grim humour, this is surpassed by a bleak single-line comment on one of the graves at Tombstone's 'Boot Hill':

> He called Bill Smith a liar.

When all's said and done, however, for callous mirth combined with cheerful obscenity, the prize must go to the Somerset village of Bampton; for the parish church there has a plaque in memory of a parish clerk's son who was killed by a falling icicle:

> Bless my I.I.I.I.
> Here he lies
> In a sad Pickle

Killed by an Icicle
In the Year 1776.

* * *

The origin of the word 'Gordano' is obscure. One explanation goes that the word stems from a combination of the Anglo-Saxon 'Gar' (a triangular spear) and 'Dene' (valley): a triangular-headed valley. Another traces its ancestry to the Saxon word 'Gyrwa' (fenny land). But James Hill, dismissing such whimsies, plumps firmly for it being a Scottish family name—Gordino or Gordoun in the original form. Yet another alternative is that it is a corruption of 'Gunni', the Danish lord of the manor at the time of Edward the Confessor.

The prefix 'Clapton' would also appear to be Saxon. 'Clappa was a King of Bernicia, and there was an Osgod Clappa who was father-in-law of Tofig Pruda (1064).' Walton, similarly, is Saxon and signifies 'Wild-Town', while Weston or 'West-Town' is self-evident.

THE NORTHERN LEVELS

A footpath from Clevedon parish church leads round to the north side of Wain's Hill, and, projecting from a ledge, is a blunt thumb of limestone overhanging the cliffs. Below, dirty grey breakers tumble and somersault and smash themselves to snow:

> Break, break, break
> On they cold grey stones O sea...

These famous lines, by Tennyson, composed in Lincolnshire, are said to refer to this spot. Whether they do or not, they are definitely about Clevedon and Hallam.

Ascending the hill, if one looks back, a fine view of the bay and the Channel fills one's field of vision. From here, or even more so, Church Hill, Clevedon looks as good as Polperro or some other agreeable spot: the rows of brightly-painted Regency houses on the seafront, backed by tiers of taller later buildings, huddle up to a samphire-capped bluff of rock; projecting from this, in a series of fragile arches, extends the pier, to end in the clean break of the fallen section; beyond, the flimsy pavilion unsteadily surveys the shift and glitter of moving tides.

Yet this does not conjure up the total effect, as the rows of houses are interspersed with trees, shrubs and miniature copses, and it is these founts of greenery, adding tone and softening the brickwork, which lend the scene an extra dimension of depth and opacity.

To the south, tall mock-Tudor villas perch on the crags of Hangstone Quarry and blearily survey a tractless expanse of housing estates and willow-fringed dykes and ditches.

* * *

A nucleus of older buildings, including Tennyson House, surrounds the church, and, in the garden of one of these, is the tiny wrecked cottage which was once held out to be the spot where Coleridge and Sara hung their Aeolian Harp and Hartley was born. Some of the details still fit; for instance, the jasmin and myrtle growing outside, the sound of the waves from the nearby pill; the situation occupying a hollow in the hill, a 'quiet dell', as it was referred to. What probably disqualifies it is its proximity to the parish church. No poet could have resisted alluding to this venerable chunk of masonry if it had been so close to his own home. And, of course, it is frightfully small.

The path that engirdles Wain's Hill finally emerges at Clevedon Pill. This, especially in winter, is a desolately appealing spot. Here the grassy levels fade into bronze and copper reeds, sand, shingle and mud. The horizon is low and punctured only by the masts of ships, and, in the distance, Middle Hope points a dark finger at the slithering tide.

In dull light and bad weather, the landscape here, in its dreary emptiness, seems almost lunar. Dull greens and greys blend and blur, and a misty indistinctness softens everything. Only the river stands out, a huge silver eel wriggling between banks of elephant-coloured mud. Once this spot was a minor harbour. During the nineteenth century, three regular trading vessels, plying between here and Newport loaded with coal from Llantwit and Lydney, accounted for Clevedon's fleet. They varied in size from 50 to 90 and 100 tons, and two of them were described as 'dandy-rigged'.

Commercially this creek is no longer used. One of the last crafts to dock here was the *Bessie* in 1934, carrying a load of gravel for a nearby housing estate. This small Barnstaple ketch was to conclude its history far from its mild West Country origins. After a bout of trading in the Mediterranean, her pilot, while heading for Dar-es-Salaam, drove her aground on a Red Sea reef, and savage and acquisitive natives stripped her of all her trophies and left her gutted hull to bake in the sun.

But the Pill was, strictly speaking, the knacker's yard for many handsome vessels. The small harbour was used for shipbreaking: the *Thornbill*—a Canadian-built ship of 1,068 tons; the old Aberdovey schooner, the *Sarah Davies*; the iron paddle steamer, the *Velindra*; softwood ships from New Brunswick—the *Reliance*, *Fines* and *Vernon*, all met their end at Clevedon. At low tide, waterlogged old hulks can still be seen marooned on the mudflats.

A sea wall follows the coast to Worlebury and the masonry is thickly coated with bitumen and angled so as to minimise the pounding it receives from each incoming tide. Eastward, drab, uninviting meadows are slashed into squares and rectangles by innumerable dykes and rhynes. Hedges are few, and so are trees, for they impede the maintenance of the ditches.

The wall itself is breached by two waterways: the tiny Land Yeo and a large drainage-channel, which, after lying stationary as a long metal bar, gurgles beneath sluice gates, stumbles over a small ledge to reach the Channel in a pretty burst of foam.

*   *   *

To the south-west, on rich loamy soil, is the village of Kenn. In the church of Saint John, there is a tablet to Sir Nicholas Stalling who died in 1605. This stalwart fellow was 'Gentleman Usher and Dayly Waiter of our Late Sovereign, of famous memory, Queen Elizabeth, and afterwards to our dread Sovereign lord, King James'. The building has a small Norman tower and a pyramid roof; the registers date from 1540.

The celebrated Bishop Ken was a descendant of an ancient family who were seated at Kenn Court from the reign of Edward II. He was one of the seven bishops who opposed James II's declaration of indulgences; for which piece of impertinence he was awarded a suite in the Tower of London.

Later he was to provoke William of Orange. Despite his rough treatment at the hands of James, he refused to transfer his oath of loyalty to the new sovereign. Thus he was deprived of the bishopric of Bath and Wells, and, during his years of exile and poverty, was put up at Naish House in Wraxall. His career, however, revived after the Restoration. Charles II was not in the least perturbed by Ken's devotional crustiness, but found it endearing. As a Prebendary at Winchester, he refused to give up his home to Nell Gwynne, the King's mistress, during the latter's visit to the city. So impressed was Charles by this snub that he decided, if ever the opportunity arose, he should restore to Ken his old title—'Who shall have Bath and Wells, but Dr Ken, the little black fellow who refused his lodging to poor Nelly.'

Nowadays the sinuous M5 snakes past Kenn and distracts from the village's individuality. The hamlet has a friendly familiar appellation, and the cluster of cottages, edged by apple-orchards and clumps of alder and willow, confirm this impression. Once a Youth Hostel stood here, but Kenn proved such an off-the-beaten-track-Cinderella-village that is custom was inadequate to justify its continued maintenance.

The Drum and Monkey, formerly the Rose and Crown, is a popular pub not far from the village. No longer is it, however, the exclusive demise of white-smocked cider-imbibing Falstaffs, who, clenching pitchforks in their hands, lumber across the bar mumbling ingenious blasphemies. These types, if they ever did exist outside BBC 2 serials, have long since croaked their last. Various gin-and-Jag and pint-and-Sprite sets congregate here, and the tone of their voices, plus the content of their repartee, contributes to an atmosphere of extraordinary vapidity.

* * *

The fields at Kenn, affording luscious pasture for cows, look sweet, green and peaceful, but they were once the scene of a macabre and brutal ritual. Some 150 years ago, when cider was cheap, plentiful and potent, the authorities were distressed by the growing incidents of hooliganism and vandalism in the county. Probably it amounted to little more than the poor and the unemployed impotently railing against the ruling classes obliviousness to their plight. Nevertheless, the latter decided that, by taking harsh measures against lawbreakers, they might curb such expressions of unrest.

This was the general background to an ill-tempered grudge which resulted in Kenn being the scene of the last public hanging in the West Country. The crime was arson. Three mows of wheat had been set alight at Yew Tree Farm, Kenn, the property of Mr Benjamin Poole.

The three men held collectively responsible for the crime were Richard Clarke, aged 17; John Rowley, aged 32; and William Wall, aged 35, a married man with seven children, the eldest of whom was 13 years of age.

It was Congresbury Fair Day, and the three prisoners were led from their cells in Ilchester gaol to the village of Kenn, over forty miles away. By about half-past ten they arrived at the hamlet. The gallows had been erected and bore a notice underlining the nature of their misdeed—'For firing stacks.'

This pathetic event was held by the country folk to be something on the lines of a royal wedding or circus performance, and from Nailsea, Clevedon, Weston and Portishead, they hurried to the spot until, it was estimated, about ten thousand people were massed in and around the field.

Instead of being swiftly and discreetly dispatched to eternity, the men were used as actors in a weird morality pantomine. In the first place, they were not ushered into the field under a moderate guard, but their approach was incorporated into a pompous and flatulent pageant.

At the head of the parade was the Chief Constable on horseback. He was followed up the rear by a hundred special constables on foot, with staves, and the High Sheriff (Mr E. Broderipp). Behind these, a carriage rattled along containing the magistrates: Messrs Roworth, J. Pigott (Brockley) and Harford (Barley-wood, Wrington). The Rev. Valentine, chaplain, accompanied grimly clutching his Bible.*

To the three condemned men, it must have seemed that the whole mighty arsenal of Somerset justice had gathered to bid them farewell.

Yet there were more to come, for, behind them, followed a party of javelin men, another company with halberts and, finally, the prison 'caravan', on which they themselves, guarded by the governor of the gaol (Mr Hardy), the executioner and his assistants, were transported.

Nor does this indicate the full extent of the procession, as there were further troops of javelin men, tenants of the High Sheriff, and fifty constables on foot. When the detachment reached Kenn, a funeral knell was tolled, the cavalcade halted and the magistrates left their carriage.

Rowley was the first to be put before them. He was eloquent in his condemnation of his fellow-culprit, Wall, who, indeed, does appear to have been the devil's advocate in this affair—'Wall planned the burning of the wheat . . . He told us we were fools if we didn't set the mows on fire . . . We wouldn't have done it if it hadn't been for him . . . When he got back from Bristol, he said he hoped Mr Poole as well as him was £20 out of pocket . . .' This last statement referred to a fine which had been imposed upon Wall, at Poole's instigation, for selling cider without a licence.

At one point, the sisters of Wall and Rowley interrupted the proceedings, begging the High Sheriff to allow them permission to speak to their brothers. This request was, firmly but gently, denied. He, apparently, considered that such filial exchanges of affection as would have taken place would distract the men from the contemplation of the solemn ordeal they were about to undergo.

---

* This account has been adapted, and, in parts, taken verbatim from a contemporary newspaper report.

The men were released from their fetters, and, accompanied by the chaplain, mounted the scaffold. They knelt, as the chaplain requested, and intoned the litany, each of them holding a prayer book—'O Lamb of God that taketh away the sins of the world, have mercy upon us.'

Wall was the first to be pinioned. Rising to face the magistrates, he said—'I hope, gentlemen, you will please forgive my poor wife and children. Lord, have mercy upon me.' Rowley was brisk and taciturn—'I have nothing to say. I hope they will take warning from us.' Wall's mind, smitten with remorse and sorrow, suddenly started preying upon the events that culminated in the firing of the stacks—'I should not have been here had I not opened my cider shop. Had I harkened to my wife, I should not have come to this. She always persuaded me not to keep a cider shop. Lord, forgive me for all my sins.'

Poor Clarke, the youngest of the malefactors, could only despairingly echo this sentiment—'Cider has been the ruin of us all!'

At 12.10 the caps were pulled down over the faces of the three condemned men, as they continued crying out—'Lord have mercy upon us. Christ, have mercy upon us.'

A signal was given. The wagon supporting the platform upon which they stood was drawn away, and their noosed bodies jerked downwards—

> It is sweet to dance to violins
>   When Love and Life are fair:
> To dance to flutes, to dance to lutes,
>   Is delicate and rare:
> But it is not sweet with nimble feet
>   To dance upon the air!

* * *

Still further south, and bordered by the meanders of the Yeo, is the village of Kingston Seymour. This is a large parish and consists mostly of rich grassland. Formerly it was prone to flooding, and in the fifteenth-century church are tablets recording disasters of earlier times, notably on January 20th, 1606, when, owing to the erosion of the sea-banks, the Channel waters surged across the fields for ten successive days; and, again in 1703, when a violent tempest did the same, submerging the land to a height of five feet, sweeping away cattle, sheep, corn and hay.

In the chancel is an altar-piece painted by Smirke and presented by J. H. Smyth Pigott of Brockley Hall. It represents the transfiguration as it was engraved for Macklin's edition of the Bible.

No brilliant witticisms sparkle amidst the gravestones, but connoisseurs of the comic-grotesque might find something to treasure in the epitaph of a certain J. H.

> He was universally beloved in the circle of
> His acquaintances; but united

> In his death the esteem of all,
> Namely, by bequeathing his remains.

Preposterous conceit? Morbid sentimentality? Neither really. In J. H.'s day, corpses were treated with far more reverence and affection than contemporary fashion would hold delicate. By bequeathing to his friends his mortal casing, J. H. was endowing them with the most tangible souvenir of his physical presence possible.

J. H.'s companion in death, a certain J. E., takes a grim relish in the fact that others will follow him (her) on that long and unitinerated journey:

> I long in pain and sickness lay
> Till Christ did summon me away.
> My debt is paid my grave you see
> Wait but a while you'll follow me.

Kingston village is a pretty huddle of cottages, modern bungalows and large farmhouses. What was its most interesting building, Kingston Manor House, is no longer to be seen. This mansion was attached to the rectory and erected in the reign of Edward IV; his badge, the Rose en Soleil, was mounted on the front of the fabric. It was designed in the form of an H, and, at the time when Rutter was writing, was still in a sound state of repair, with an open-ribbed roof and projecting porches, the interior of one of which contained the entrance to the chief apartments of the manor. Fire destroyed this house over a century ago.

* * *

In the vicinity of Kingston the River Yeo wriggles to the sea. In many ways an undistinguished stream, from its source at Blagdon it trickles through a broad shallow valley, past the villages of Wrington and Congresbury, down to a green and monotonous plain. There it passes a Roman villa, and, depositing mud and silt, grubbily winds along its estuary—senile almost from the start. However, from a fisherman's point of view, it has its consolations (brown trout, grayling, roach, rudd), and it does seem to have found a laureate in the person of Ralph Elton:

> When will we ride on our trolley again
> To bump and wobble through the happy hours
> Singing to the guttering candle's sweet whipcrack
> Rolling through the scented laurel bowers?
>
> Or sail in our home-built scow
> Flat bottomed with red-blanket sail
> Along the steep-banked Yeo
> Our secret sea?

Around here it is true fen country, and, in fact, in the whole of Britain, excluding East Anglia, there is no greater area of low lying land.

The Somerset Levels affect some people powerfully. They possess a distinct atmosphere: the bluegrey skies with their pillowy cloud-outlines, the straight willow-fringed roads, the occasional farm-dwellings, the gulls floating on the tide like paper boats or restlessly hovering and whining, the crisscrossing rhynes and droveways, the furred and scratchy outlines of hedges and brambles, the swelling green bruise of the Mendips lording above the flood plain with the whole outlook softened by a watery sash of mist—all this gently impresses the mind. It is true marsh country and exudes timelessness and melancholy.

At the coastal verges, adjoining the Yeo estuary, there is a noticeably elaborate stretch of sea wall, broad, spacious, gently sloping, with a double platform to disperse tidal impact. The reason for this relatively complex structure lies in the differing character of wave movement between the southern and northern half of the coastal belt. For instance, west of Bridgwater Bay, the tide runs almost parallel with the shore, but at the estuary of the Parrett, it comes in at right angles, and it is this northward bend of the coastline which renders it more potentially erosive. Also, the swift movement of the waters being checked by the obstacle of the shore itself, it favours the formation of spitheads and sand-bars, one of the most geomorphologically interesting of which can be seen at Stert Island. The progress of material, held in suspension by the waves, is abruptly halted, and the sediment percolates to the bed of the estuary, as it once, in previous years, inundated the poorly-drained countryside. Souvenirs of those days can be seen along the wall at Kingston in the form of crude stone tablets, scrawled with initials and planted in the turfy embankment by men who were engaged in the construction of these defences.

The original architects of Somerset's sea-walls are still something of a mystery. It has been suggested that the Romans, experts as they were in constructing walls, roads, dykes and drainage schemes, had a hand in early embankment building, but the evidence relating to this matter is insubstantial, relying heavily on a single inscribed stone on the Welsh coast and the remains of a villa excavated in 1884 at Yatton. The latter was situated at a level below that of the high tide, and it is unlikely that, were it under threat of regular flooding, the Romans would have selected such a position. Critics of the contention state that the land stood higher then and the villa's site was far from precarious.

* * *

On the south bank of the Yeo lies Wick Saint Lawrence. The track of the old Weston, Clevedon and Portishead Light Railway once crossed the road into the village, and cracked and leaning piers sprouting from the creamy mud are all that remain of the old iron bridge that once carried the track across the river.

The W.C.P.L.R.* which flourished from about 1907 to 1940, was not one of those grimly efficient institutions. It was, in fact, a sleepy and casual service embodying the best West Country traditions of placidity and

---

* Referred to by wags as the 'Canadian Pacific' or 'Fred Karno's Railway'.

reflectiveness: the idlest of whims and the flimsiest of fancies tended to ride roughshod over the exigencies of its timetable. The driver, after warning the guard with three sharp blasts of his whistle, would stop the train to cull some mushrooms from a nearby meadow or exchange pleasantries with a farmer of his acquaintance. On arriving at Weston, the mushrooms would be fried on a shovel with bacon and consumed. Children would get out at level crossings to pick flowers and refuse to return to their carriages when the train was about to start up. Would-be acrobats would contrive to gather blackberries from hedgerows while the locomotive was still moving. Vagaries such as these attracted the amused comment of a Welsh newspaper reporter:

> Among other novelties that delight visitors to Weston-super-Mare and Clevedon these holiday times, are the wonderful ways of the Weston, Clevedon and Portishead Railway, whereon time is no object, and running schedules are regarded as vain things. One day last week, the so-called 3.45 train left Clevedon for Weston, and skimmed along for four or five miles, ignoring the claims of intermediate stations for something like a quarter of an hour. Then it transpired that an angry clergyman, who was travelling with his worthy helpmate, and booked for the intermediate station which had been left a few miles in the rear. The error of the train in skipping that important station had, therefore, grievously disappointed and discommoded him. The railway officials, however, were quite equal to the occasion. To the amazement of all and sundry they simply ordered the train to push back again over the single line to the station some miles behind near Clevedon, and in this manner soothed the reverend gentleman.

Railway regulations were equally bizarre. Whether male juveniles—contrary to modern sociological findings—were more precocious in those days, one would hesitate to say; certainly some of the W.C.P.L.R. stipulations remain inscrutable:

> Except by express permission of the guard of the train, a person of the male sex above or apparently above, the age of eight years, shall not travel, or attempt to travel or remain in any compartment of a carriage marked or notified as being reserved or appropriated for the exclusive use of persons of the female sex.

Except for the odd rusting girder, stretches of earthwork and scattered concrete ramps, little tangible evidence of the W.C.P.L.R. remains today. Perhaps the most substantial souvenir is in the Yeo estuary itself. The wharf onto which the coal from South Wales was unloaded and transferred by steam crane to the trucks is, excluding some portions of collapsed decking, still standing, and, at its seaward end, rails can be seen sunk into the concrete stop blocks.

Curiously enough, this dreary little harbour, going by the name of Slutspill in the seventeenth century, once enjoyed regular trade, and there is a tradition which states that ships once sailed up the Yeo as far as Congresbury.

Archaeologists have tentatively identified an outbuilding of the Roman villa as a boathouse.

Yet what strikes the stranger about this region is its air of drowsy remoteness. Wick, especially when it is enveloped in a mild heat haze, has an almost hypnotically peaceful quality, like the hamlet into which Rip Van Winkle descended after his long sleep. In the 1900s a traveller passing this way excites genuine interest:

> Rarely the stranger in these parts meets any other wayfarers than farming folk, and the children of Wick St Lawrence at the sight of him stand stock-still with fingers in mouths, quaint figures of combined curiosity and shyness, clad in the old rustic way in homely clothes and clean 'pinners'.

In 1636, somewhere to the north of this neighbourhood, a crew of Algerian priates landed. These swarthy and sinister brigands kidnapped some of the local parishioners and made off with them to sea. The fate of the women has been the source of some speculation, and it has been suggested that they ended their years in a harem for the anthological delectation of some smirking sultan. If so, this must have proven an exotic respite from tugging cows' teats or scraping dung off their husband's boots.

* * *

To return to Wick village, it does not appear to be a spot which has branded an indelible impression on many minds, although possibly some American emigrant, who was formerly a native of the place, might have fond memories of ambling English lanes and of the sweet-rotten smells of numerous cowsheds. Collinson, in his eighteenth-century survey, referred to Wick as a small village situated by the sea in a 'woody flat' of very rich pasture, five miles north-west of Congresbury. Earlier still, John Leland, who had visited the hamlet in the reign of Henry VIII, did not enthuse over its situation—'Banwell standeth not very holsomly and Wick worse. The fennes be almost at hand. Wood meately good about them.'

No trace of the wood referred to is in evidence today, but the allusion would seem to indicate that the village stood on a section of dried-out fenland. The marshy parts had been absorbed and begun to support mature woodland. These forested areas may have been formerly extensive—'Woodspring' is a name close by.

In the Perpendicular style, the parish church of Saint Lawrence has a beautifully-carved pulpit of freestone from Woodspring Priory. The dedication is interesting. Saint Lawrence was the Archdeacon of Rome during the persecution of Valerian. He was ordered by the authorities to surrender to them all the treasures of the church. He agreed to this demand, and, one day later, he appeared before a tribunal attended by beggars, lepers, the blind, crippled and poor. 'These,' he riposted, 'are the treasures of the church.' The authorities, on receiving this insolence, ordered that he should be burnt on a gridiron. This instruction was duly obeyed. Lawrence, who, when the occasion merited it, could turn a neater line in dialogue than the combined wits of

Groucho Marx and Oscar Wilde, at one point during his ghastly ordeal remarked to his executioners—'Turn me, I am done on this side.' This digression would appear peripheral to the present study, but, in actual fact, it is relevant, as, not many years ago, a newspaper columnist of some local standing, enquired of his readers if they could tell him, why, whenever the sun was prickly and sweltering, old Somerset gaffers would exclaim 'Lawrence!' and then remove their jerkins.

The sea no longer invades this area. In the year 1304, in the reign of Edward I, its destructive powers were curbed by the formation of sea-walls, dykes and drains. Yet, despite these measures, in the year of the great flood (1607)*, a high spring tide, agitated by a strong wind, broke over the defences and inundated large areas of the countryside. And this epitaph, inscribed on a tablet in Wick parish church, testifies to the dangers of wandering about the mudflats and salt marshes at high tide:

To the memory of JAMES MORSS, of this parish, yeoman, who dy'd November ye 25th 1730, aged 38 years.

> Save me, O God, the mighty waters role
> With near Approaches, even to my soul:
> Far from dry ground, mistaken in my course,
> I stick in mire, brought hither by my horse.
> Thus vain I cry'd to God, who only saves:
> In death's cold pit I lay ore whelm'd with waves.

---

* There appears to be some divergence of opinion concerning the date of the great flood. Most sources agree on the day and the month, January 20th, but regarding the year, some North Somerset parishes opt for 1606. Kingston Seymour church has a tablet recording the flood to have taken place on this date, the fourth year in the reign of James I, and this has been widely accepted by many books. The overwhelming bulk of information, however, points to the year 1607.

WOODSPRING

BEYOND the village of Wick, rising like a blunt grey thumb above the clumps of elms and fields of thick silky grasses, the tower of Woodspring Priory prods the horizon. Even today this mellow ruin has mercifully few visitors, and its setting remains an enclave of silence and serenity. If approached from the north, it is necessary to ford the tiny pill of the Banwell river and traverse the edge of a field in order to reach the main footpath to the priory.

The initial impression is of a haphazard cluster of buildings, fringed by glossy lawns and casual flowerbeds, huddled around a graceful tower, the Perpendicular windows of which have been restored by the Landmark Trust that now owns it. Predominantly squirrel-grey Carboniferous Limestone, here and there the walls have been patched and refaced with Dolomite from Clevedon and Oolite from Dundry, and the warmer honey tones of these materials contrast gently with their setting. A chimney stack adjoins the tower reminding the purist that the edifice has been used for secular purposes for as long a period as it was occupied by monks.

The story of this Augustinian establishment is fascinating. Allegedly Reginald FitzUrse— one of the murderers of Thomas a Becket—first founded a chapel of expiation on this site. It would appear that, after sheathing his sword in the flesh of the Blessed Archbishop, his own conscience was gored by the burning horn of eternal damnation. Certainly the killing had been a gutty and brutal affair. 'They,' wrote John Salisbury, 'cut off the crown of his head, which had been dedicated to God by the unction of sacred chrism, and (which is horrifying to relate) scraped out the brains of the dead man with their murderous swords and most barbarously scattered them together with blood and bone upon the paving stones.'

Yet this explanation, superficially plausible, is not backed up by hard

IN LOVING MEMORY OF
JANE MARIA PERCEVAL
WHO DESIGNED THE
CHVRCHYARD CROSS &
THE ABOVE WINDOW &
ADDED MVCH TO THE ENRICHMENT
OF THIS CHVRCH WHICH ACCORDING
TO LOCAL TRADITION WAS ORIGINALLY
FOVNDED BY HER ANCESTOR ASCELIN
PERCEVAL IN THE 12TH CENTVRY
SHE DIED 9TH OCTOBER 1922
IN HER 90TH YEAR
THIS TABLET WAS ERECTED BY HER
SISTER FREDERICA FANNY & HER BROTHER
ALFRED SPENCER PERCEVAL 1932

Weston-in-Gordano. Commemorative Plaque to the Percevals.

ton-in-Gordano.
Perceval Cross.

Weston-in-Gordano.
The Perceval Window.

The Winter Monu[ment]
the interior of
St Michael's, Cla[pton]

The M5 Motorway,
the Gordano Valley.

Clapton Court,
the Gordano Vall[ey]
Built by Sir Willi[am]
Arthur in 1325 a[nd]
enlarged and deve[l]
oped by Richard
Arthur in 1450.

Pier, Clevedon, August 1975. Built on an
'...enwork' plan, the pier was cunningly
...structed from Barlow rails—formerly used
...the South Wales Railway.

Adelaide House, the Promenade, Clevedon.
Typical Regency building.

...vedon. The Pill.

above: The Clock,
the Triangle, Clevedon.

left: The Bandstand,
Elton Road, Clevedon.

Coleridge Cottag(e)
Old Church Roa(d)
Clevedon.

Clevedon sea wall with its forbidding notice.

The massive cur(ved) stretch of the sea wall.

Kingston Seymour. The old Manor House—burned down over a century ago.

St. Lawrence.
tump of an
t cross, once
ng twenty five
gh, occupies a
nent position in
lage centre.

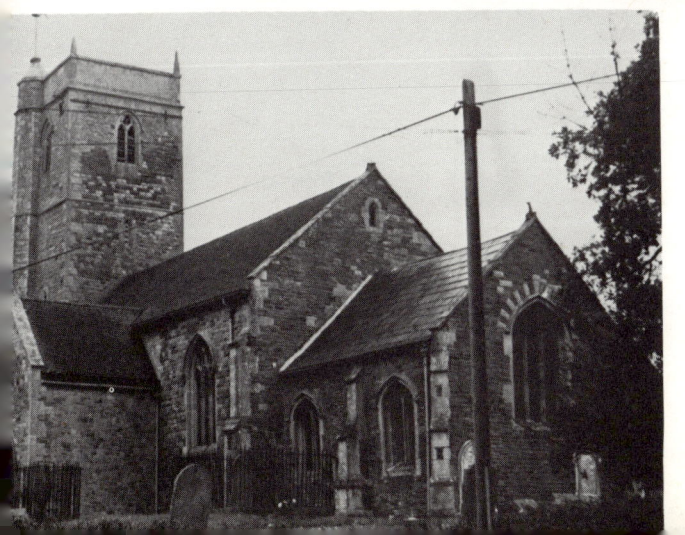

Wick St. Lawrence. The Parish Church.

Woodspring.
Mr Richard Crook, the caretaker of the Priory, stands against the pierced quatrefoil parapet.

Woodspring Priory, the Tower, is 65 feet high and is ascended by an octagonal stair turret. It once had square corner pinnacles.

Woodspring. The Well.

...l Station, Walton Bay.

The Gordano Valley from Clapton Church.

...ichael's Church, Clapton.

The Black Horse, Clapton.

The Old Rectory, Walton-in-Gordano.

St Paul's Church, Walton-in-Gordano.

Tomb of Richard Perceval, the Parish Church, Weston-in-Gordano.

documentary evidence, and although FitzUrse undoubtedly owned 'Worspring' in 1172, whether he inaugurated the chapel that stood there in the early years of the thirteenth century is an open question. The popular, though by no means established, date given for the formation of the priory is 1210. In that year or thereabouts, William de Courtenay—grandson, on the maternal side, of FitzUrse—wrote a letter to Jocelin, Bishop of Bath, declaring his intention to found a monastic house for the order of the monks of St Augustine, to be dedicated to God, the Virgin Mary, and Blessed Martyr Thomas. De Courtenay himself, in the document, makes no mention of attempting to expunge any guilt he felt he may have inherited. Nevertheless, he does specifically refer to the welfare of the souls of his wife, father, mother and his 'ancestors'—as if they were touched by some hereditary sin. Possibly this is to read too much into it, but, on this evidence alone, a reasonably strong case could be made for the expiation theory. Why, for instance, out of all the numerous alternatives, select St Thomas the Martyr of Canterbury as the principal dedicatee?

The actual structure itself—compared with the extravaganzas at Glastonbury and Tintern—is of modest dimensions. On either side of the approach to the priory, supported by stone piers, are shields, one of which exhibits the 'five wounds', and the other a chevron between three bugle horns stringed. The Perpendicular tower is of two stages, with large traceried windows in the belfry storey; on the south side is a stair turret with pyramidal capping, and the lower stage has fan-traceried vaulting. The nave and the north aisle were converted into a farmhouse, and a large stone pulpit—said to be the finest in the country—was extracted from the building and now occupies the parish church at Wick St Lawrence.

To the south is the infirmary, a plain sturdy building of the early fifteenth century, with good medieval timberwork on view in the roof and transomed windows of two lights.

North of the priory is a well-preserved Monastic barn. This has a bold south transept with angle buttresses, one of which displays a disfigured coat of arms. At the east end of the barn is a well fed by a perpetual spring. One would assume this feature to account for the name of the priory, but, as is often the case, James Hill has different ideas:

> Woodspring would seem naturally to mean 'spring in the wood'. But other things spring beside founts of living water. Spring is the season of bursting buds. And a spring, or sprinca, is a young wood or plantation. As the original spelling is Worspring, and as Worle is Worla, a personal name hard by, Worspring is probably Worla-spring.'

* * *

Nearby the promontory of Middle Hope swims bleakly out to sea. Bald, windswept, rocky, inhospitable, it rises to a modest height of 162 feet and lacks the grandeur of Brean Down. On the map its outline resembles a razor-billed duckling or an alligator's head. Yet, to the geologist, it has its points of interest, for injected into its limestone bedrock, are lava flows and tuffs.

On what could be loosely termed the elbow of this peninsula the Navy researches underwater mining devices, and it is possible on certain occasions to witness the fruits of their activities. To watch the grey waters abruptly jet upwards in a roaring volcano of foam and spray can be most entertaining. Visitors, however, should not attempt to explore this area too thoroughly: access to certain parts is strictly prohibited.

The western part, on the other hand, with its finely-curving bay and Swallow Cliff rising to a graceful symmetrical cone and looking considerably higher than its actual elevation, is owned by the National Trust and said to be haunted by the ghost of John Crock, the ploughboy from Wick St Lawrence.

This little known—yet decidedly odd—Somerset legend is connected with the phenomena called 'ogre fumes.' These were wisps of marsh gas which, according to folklore, used to intimidate country folk by assuming a variety of spectral forms: a black dog, a large stallion with one eye in the centre of his head*, and, sometimes, the figure of the Devil himself. There were two ways of exorcising these apparitions: one was by reciting a rather long-winded and inscrutable Latin catechism, the other by appeasing the Devil by promising to perform at least one bad deed during the following week. The snag was that once a man or woman had agreed to that last condition, the ogre fumes would appear with increasing regularity; and this is, in fact, what happened to poor John Crock.

While he was fording the Banwell river one evening, the black dog appeared. Terrified, Crock agreed to steal some grain from his master. The dog then vanished. After he had performed the theft, he was crossing the same patch of moor again when the ogre fumes started wreathing upwards from the fenny land. This time they took the form of the one-eyed stallion who informed Crock that, in order to fully satisfy the Devil's requirements, he would have to perpetrate another crime: namely to manufacture evidence against the wife of a local priest to make it appear that she was a witch. Crock agreed; and the woman was eventually burnt. From that time onwards, the ogre fumes would constantly appear, throwing up their grotesque shapes; and, to make them disperse, he found himself goaded into performing a whole series of ghastly acts: burning down farms, slaughtering horses and swine, and, finally and most brutally, killing his wife and only son. After this last deed, sick of mind and crazy with remorse, he ran across the fields to Swallow Cliff on Middle Hope promontory and flung himself over.

> Neath Swallowcliffe
> Where cold seas role
> John Crock met death:
> Pray for his soul.
> Devil, blackdog, one-eyed stallion,
> Trouble him no more: his body's carrion.

This effusion, composed by John Bowler, the eccentric poet-stonemason of Woolvers Hill, was inscribed on a tablet above the cliff-face in 1816; and, five years later, destroyed by two local yahoos. They, after imbibing many

---

* An image employed by Fuseli.

gallons of a famous local product, uprooted the stone and hurled it over the Cliff where it shattered. The verse itself was recorded in one of the notebooks of Lisle Bowles.

One other feature of interest may be mentioned in connection with Middle Hope, or, to use its older coinage, Saint Thomas's Head, and this concerns a pile of loose stones called 'Castle Mound'. Occupying the western tip of the headland, they are alluded to by Mr George Bennett, a Banwell antiquarian, whose painstaking and detailed notes (beginning in 1804 and ending with his death in 1834) contain a number of unique observations relating to the locality. It is thought that they constitute the remains of one of the three round towers—the others being sited at Uphill and Weston—erected in the reign of Henry VIII for purposes of coastal defence. All three of these structures were equipped with two cannons and served to temper the enthusiasm of the Spanish Armada and other aspiring sea-wolves.

* * *

South of Middle Hope urban development begins. The smooth and regular shores of Sand Bay are lined by rows of gaily painted bungalows with names like 'Tregarwith', 'Overtones' and 'The Ritz'. This spot can be unattractive at low water when pungent and salt-smelling reeds accumulate along the tideline, together with the tangled bladderwrack. Here also, Spartina Grass, like a dingy brown stain, is encroaching upon the sandy areas to the south.

In winter the Bay is transformed into a scene of windswept loneliness. Raw, deserted, colourless, in the weakening light walking along the embankment above the sandy beach one has the sensation of a sentry patrolling some desolate military outpost on the shores of the frozen Baltic. Everything is shuttered, bleak and lifeless. With the holiday chalets locked and abandoned, all smiles, signboards and attempts at summer gaiety dismantled, the place seems utterly robbed of purpose. What remains is a huge dreary inlet overshadowed by the great amorphous stain of Worlebury. No charabancs sweep past to dispatch excited parties of adults and children to Pontin's Holiday Camp. No one—apart from the occasional stray—ventures out on the sand. Even the lighted bungalows appear somehow barren and private, not secure units in an integral community, but just set down, row after blank-faced row—cold, rectangular and self-absorbed.

The promenade is as bare as the blade of a knife. As for the beach, it looks like an eerie junkyard. Huge logs, bleached and bone-dry, festooned with seaweed; rubber tyres worn smooth with usage; rusting oil drums; decomposing fibreboard panels; vivid chlorine blue detergent bottles: all these articles—the lingering rejects of our civilisation—are slung together, as if in some grotesque modern sculpture, to serve as a reminder of what, when everything else is obliterated, might finally survive of modern technology. These, our waste products, we bequeath to the future as the past has bequeathed Woodspring Priory to us.

On November 4th, 1959, drifts of fine light-grey sand were found overlying the brown quartz sand of the beach. 'It proved to be fly ash, minute glassy globules, blown out of the chimneys of some electricity station fired by pulverised fuel.' The globules contained gas bubbles which enabled them to float on the sea before the wind and currents forced them to accumulate on the shore.

* * *

Two miles outside Weston is Kewstoke. The name, it is believed, is derived from the Celtic word 'Kewch' (boat) and 'Stoke' (station). So Kew Stoke: boat-station or 'harbour'. Another less plausible explanation ascribes the name of the village to Saint Kew—an obscure Celtic saint—having built a chapel on the nearby hillside.

In the early English and Perpendicular style, the church of Saint Paul consists of a chancel, nave, south porch and a western tower with a pierced trefoil parapet, and an octagonal spired turret at the south-east angle. A reliquary was discovered here in 1850, at the back of which was found a cup containing traces of blood—allegedly that of Thomas a Becket.* This is now at Taunton Museum and is thought to have come from the nearby priory at Woodspring.

Yet the most striking, if not the most architecturally felicitous, building in the vicinity is the Convalescent Home. Set in spacious grounds with a driveway broad enough to take a Boeing, this creamy-pink edifice resembles one of those grandiose hotels at Nice or Monaco and contrasts garishly with the bottle-green slopes of Worlebury Hill. The tourist, who finds his senses blunted by the dazzle and magnificence of this dinosaur, might like to wander a little inland and find solace in the elegant rusticity of Newton Farm House (1710), a two-storeyed residence with wooden cross-windows and a pedimented porch.

Near the church are the Monk's Steps. Occupying a cleft in the hill, this steep limestone staircase was thought to have been linked with the harbourage at Kew Stoke and Worlebury Camp. Alternatively, it may have formed a route from Milton to Kewstoke. At the top of the steps was a chamber called the 'Cell of St Kew'. This, when excavated, was found to contain an altogether bizarre assortment of articles: a Saxon knife, a fifteenth-century spur, a sword-hilt of the Civil War, a tiny silver brooch, coins and primitive pottery. Sadly, this underground enclosure is no longer what it was: a Luftwaffe pilot, during the last war, dropped a bomb on it and drastically modified its appearance.

From the top of the steps, it is only a short walk to the Observatory in the parish of Worle. This small castellated tower, teetering near the edge of a sheer quarryface, was built around 1870. Once it was rather prettily decked up, with a wooden lantern and an ogival metal roof, but time and vandals have removed these accoutrements. To get to the lookout point, it was necessary to climb a series of ladders. Nowadays one would have to acquire the permission of whoever lives there: it has been converted into a flat.

Worle, as a village, has a few points of interest. The parish church,

* Not in the Reverend Jackson's opinion—'Becket's blood would certainly have been enclosed in a crystal monstrance, adorned with gems, the gifts of excited devotees, locked away in a shrine or subterranean safe, and displayed on festivals, and in return for lucrative fees or donations.'

Kewstoke   The Monk's Steps

dedicated to Saint Martin, has a late Norman doorway and some Elizabethan plate; the tower, surmounted by a parapet and octagonal turret, has crocketted pinnacles and contains six bells.

The parish registers bear an interesting entry for the year 1609. It concerns a certain Edward Bustle, who, by the connivance of his wife, one Humphrey Hawkins and his associate, was brutally murdered. The body, savagely mutilated, was eventually discovered by the authorities concealed in a stall: the throat had been slit, both legs chopped off, and over all of the frame were deep lacerations. A grim retribution followed. The criminals were speedily traced, and the three of them received the maximum penalty. They were conducted to Shute Shelf, the local place of execution, near Axbridge, and there they were hung in irons. Humphrey Hawkins' widow, happily, was not deprived of her conjugal rights for any considerable period by the abrupt demise of her husband. The fact that he had served as a pendant to decorate a gallow's chain did not forestall the ardours of Nicholas Pitman who married her in October of the same year. Love, like murder, will out.

* * *

The school, hard by the church, was converted out of a medieval stone barn, and the clocktower, erected by public subscription, stands as a memorial to those of the parish who lost their lives in the 1914–18 war.

An interesting footnote to Worle's history is the community's alleged aversion to members of the legal profession. On hearing the rallying signal of the famous 'Worle Drum', the inhabitants of the village would set upon any judge, lawyer, barrister, or poor solicitor's clerk, encroaching upon their domain. Their progress would be hastened by blows, duckings, kicks and other techniques of evacuative therapy.

WESTON-SUPER-MARE

FORMERLY a cluster of twenty-four fishing huts, Weston-super-Mare is the heaven to which all good inhabitants of Coronation Street fervently pray to be sent. Its hotel and accommodation facilities are impressive, and it provides for the holidaymaker a solid diet of entertainment in the way of shows, dances, bands, swimming-galas and funfairs. Licked clean by gusting westerlies, the promenade is broad and spaced out with benches and places of refreshment. Also, there is a pleasing quantity of metal on display: Victorian shelters, tricked out with spikes and tinny pagodas, the solid ironwork of the Grand Pier, the helmeted turret of the Sandringham Restaurant, the mushroom dome of the Winter Gardens Pavilion, and, less happily, miles of parked cars.

The sands themselves are fine. In the summer, they are grazed by a morose herd of donkeys that trot back and forth every five minutes with a fresh crop of juvenile passengers. The Punch and Judy Show is also a great favourite with children and adults who prefer entertainment that is intellectually undemanding.

Although mentioned in the Doomsday Record, the town as it stands is almost wholly Victorian. Amusingly enough, its very first guidebook, far from being couched in the oily euphemisms of the coventional tourist tract, was brutally candid:

> Weston does not present a very inviting appearance to the stranger. The houses, scattered mostly without arrangement, and roofed with red tile, give a character of meanness to the village; and if the stranger first enters it on a stormy day and at low water, he may perhaps feel inclined to turn his horse's head back home again.

In those early days, Weston was regarded as a rather select playground and was avidly patronised by the wealthy of Bath, Bristol, Cheltenham and Oxford. But its provincial fastidiousness has long since evaporated. Nowadays all the conventional regalia of an English seaside holiday adorns its seafront: plastic wind-shelters, weighing machines, stalls selling hamburgers, ice creams, candyfloss and the glittery breakables of the souvenir trade.

A factor which contributed to Weston's wealth and popularity was its reputation as a health resort. The air, impregnated with iodine, is supposed to alleviate various complaints. Writing on this matter, a former Medical Officer of Health listed a whole range of ailments that the town's bracing climate might help to counteract, but added that those suffering from internal haemorrhage or acute mental disorders had best select a more 'sedative' climate.

Why is this? The answer, apparently, lies in those hearty backslapping gales that cuff the solitary stroller-along-the-promenade. Levitating hats, fluttering skirts and coat-tails, they are too 'stimulating' for such serious maladies.

The winds, however, are deserving of a measure of respect, as they are the only relic of Old Weston left. Nothing else remains of that primitive fishing community, which, at the start of the nineteenth century, huddled among the sandbanks near the intertidal zone. The town itself then comprised solely of their tumbledown huts. Known familiarly as 'Auster Tenements', their inhabitants plied their trade, staking out their nets at dawn, waiting to see what legacies the tide might leave them—but speculative eyes were fixed upon them. The year was 1808, and Mr Cox, of Brockley, and Mr Richard Parsley, of Weston-super-Mare, acquired a perpetual leasehold on these properties.

Development then began in earnest. The sand-ridges were flattened and work was begun on a large hotel, to be known as Reeves' Hotel, the profits from which initially were negligible. Custom was simply inadequate. Weston had no shops, no butchers, bakers or candlestick-makers, to attract regular visitors, and it seemed that the energetic gentlemen had overplayed their hand.

Hotel life then was uneventful. Occasionally the monotony would be relieved by local artisans who would undertake the strenuous three-mile trek to Worle Brewery. There they would purchase a nine-gallon barrel of beer, and, by cart or brute strength, convey it to the hotel. Word would get around that beer was to be had that evening, and, for a night, there would be laughter and carousing before the concern would relapse back into the doldrums.

Yet, despite its rather chilly debut, the hotel stuck it out, and, eventually, other buildings followed. Mr Isaac Jacobs, of coloured glass fame, was one of the first gentlemen to erect a private residence at Weston. The house, Belvedere, may still be seen along with Sidmouth House, at its rear, which was designed to contain his offices and billiard table. Mr Christopher Kingdom, at this time, built Claremont Lodge, and a host of other building began to diversify the shoreline. To put dates on a few of these, Waterloo House went up in the year it commemorates; the neighbouring Sea View Place, in 1817; South Parade, in 1819; and the first esplanade—not the spacious present-day affair—was completed in 1826. By then Weston was truly fashionable.

From this point building after building rapidly sprang up, grey and white villa, Italianate and Gothic, neo-Classical terrace and Jacobean row, fake Tudor gable and Early English spire, they spread across the knuckles of Worlebury, over the rumpled sand-ridges as far as Uphill, inland to Worle, around the bay to Kewstoke, and the gaunt hill-backed plain was slowly transformed into Somerset's largest holiday resort.

This then gives an indication of Weston's background. As for its populace, it could be said that, to a certain extent, they reflect its architectural variety. Enter any bar in the town at random, and there may be a retired army officer shouting 'What's your poison?' across the counter, and in a corner elsewhere you may see a down-at-heel actor fresh from the labour exchange; opposite him, a student from the technical college hunched over a copy of the New Musical Express; and then, in another part of the room, a pair of young Cypriots, an Italian restaurant owner, a determinedly upright species of decaying gentility—the variety is endless. Weston, to put it in a nutshell, is a town composed of disparate odds-and-ends of people, or, to phrase it more pretentiously—of a soft-focus hierarchy: one social strata blends imperceptibly with another.

It can also be a fairly violent place: knifings and assaults occur intermittently, and the occasional murder, though rare, is not unknown. Illegitimacy, to which holidaymakers cheerfully contribute, is quite high, and the figures for church-attendance correspondingly low.

As for the general appearance of the town, it may be said that the modern does not blend very well with the old. The decor of many of the cafes tends to be garishly drab: plastic cloth seats, metal-legged tables and walls advertising the scenic delights of elsewhere. Decorated in vivid pastel shades, they seem to be still entrenched in the fifties milk-bar heyday. The buildings that do not, the office blocks and department stores, serve to emphasise the chaotic shapeless layout of the town; among the high-pitched Victorian gables and intricately decorated facades, their boxy glass-and-metal fabric appears disjointed and remote. And there is no drama in this contrast, only confusion and incongruity.

The design of the seafront, however, does much to make amends for what deficiencies are to be found within its streets and walls. First and foremost, standing near the seashore one gets an impression of space. This exhilaratingly open aspect is composed of many dramatic features: of the huge scythe-cut of the bay culminating in the uplift of Brean; of the esplanade fretted with lawns, kiosks and baroque fountains; of the gables, turrets, battlements, domes and balustrades that variegate the shore; of the horn-tip of Knightstone, with its neat decorous towers overlooking the clusters of yachts and cabin cruisers on the beach; of the Grand Pier, a gaudy-exotic fortress, secure on its black Edwardian-iron legs; of the view across the Channel, where Steepholm, a rocky cyst of an islet, and its sister, Flatholm, low, sprouting a tall stick-of-chalk lighthouse, rise like ghosts of eroded mountains between the plains of chocolatey mud and the mist-bleached horizon.

* * *

Weston's architectural highlights combine flamboyance and gloom in characteristic Victorian proportions. Facing the Marine Parade, on a site formerly known as 'Roger's Field', is the Winter Gardens. This large pavilion and dance-hall, although a pseudo-Roman sham, has an attractive formal garden round its back with lily ponds and pergolas. In Knightstone Road are two curved terraces both late classical. One of them is, nevertheless, modified by Tudor hood-moulds. But the town comes closest to the mode of architecture for which Bath is renowned in Royal Crescent, an impressive and solidly-built classical row. Yet the overall effect lacks delicacy and grace. It is heavy and ponderous and the tall paperclip-shaped arches enclosing the windows underline this impression; also, it is badly sited, in that it does not dramatically open out, but is partly tree-shrouded and obscured by walls. Oriel Terrace, in Lower Church Road, with its cross-windows and Jacobean gables, strikes the eye as pleasant enough. The design is unfussy and decoration is minimal. Both this row and the crescent date from 1847.

The Town Hall, built in the Italian style with a campanile, has an illuminated clock and stands in Walliscote Road. The building was the generous gift of Bishop Law; he erected it at the cost of £4,000 in 1856. Architectural purists, disliking its foreign overtones, maintained that it should have been built in the hackneyed English Perpendicular style, which was suffering from a furious revival at the time.

Not far away, the Odeon Cinema, like a massive block of cheese, advertises its attractions—designed by Cecil Howitt in 1934. Of more eccentric design is the Constitutional Club in the Boulevard. This penny-plain folly, in Bath stone, has a picturesque tower grafted onto its battlements, like a bit of old Heidelberg. Nearby the Technical College—a drably functional slab of concrete and plateglass—dominates the skyline with its mass and solidity; while, just a stone's throw away in Grove Park, the bronze-winged figure of Victory balances delicately on her pedestal of Portland Stone, clutching an olive branch. But the skyline around these parts is most assertively shattered by the tower of Saint John's Church. In the Early English style, the fabric was extensively rebuilt in 1824 and has a nicely whitewashed interior, with a good stained chancel window (the gift of Bishop Law) and a wrought iron screen.

Lastly, and of perhaps especial appeal to necrophiles, there is the Cemetery on the Bristol Road. This rather large boneyard covers an area of some 20 acres and affords a pleasant, if ghoulish, stroll. Built on a smooth green slope, impeccably maintained, it is open and windswept and emanates a certain grey and melancholy poetry. The best feature of this haven of rest are two grim little Poesque mortuary chapels, well-harmonised, with a spiky turret, simulated plate tracery and withdrawn forbidding air. They are connected by a bell-chamber and taper into a slender Gothic spire.

* * *

Yet, despite these glories, the seafront remains the most attractive part of the town. The bay, with its views across the Channel to Wales and the Holms, has a sweep and impressiveness unique among nearby resorts. At the southern end, opposite the Clevedon Road, is The Pool. Constructed in 1937, this swimming-bath measures 220 by 135 feet and contains 885,000 gallons of seawater. Its diving stage is considered by experts to be one of the finest in Britain, and the gradually sloping bed of the pool attains a depth of fifteen feet in the centre. Although the water is not heated, it warms up rapidly in July and August and large areas at its verges are put aside for sunbathing.

The Pool, in the warmer months, is the scene of regular Bathing Beauty Contests, a factor which makes it increasingly popular among middle-aged married men and grammar school boys. Female liberationists, referring to these events as 'cattle markets', continue to protest while leering and slack-mouthed judges assess the quality of prime beef on display.

At the junction of Regent Street and Marine Parade stands the Grand Pier, which, inevitably, brings one on to the subject of entertainments in Weston. This iron structure completed in 1904, extends for about a quarter of a mile and is forty feet wide. Unlike Clevedon's fragile arches, this pier is upheld by a dense jungle of supports and intersecting ties. Electric cars run its length in summer, and there is a balcony affording good sea views and opportunities for feeding gulls. At the seaward end is a large pavilion, a flashy castellated wedding-cake of an enclosure, providing numerous alternatives to spending one's time thriftily and creatively: a ghost train, big dipper, rifle range, hall of mirrors, crazy house, dodgem cars and slot machines.*

If the diversions of this fun palace start to pall, the conscientious visitor might care to seek refuge in the nearby Model Village, where, like Gulliver, he may rub knees with church spires and crush humble cottages underfoot. If, however, he favours the bulbous stares of tropical fish, parrot's expletives and the bonhomie of apes, he might drop in at the Aquarium and Zoo. Bored by this, he could—if he be of a persistent nature—wait until evening and then patronise the Old Time Dancing. If, after an hour or so, he does not succumb to the spectacle of revolving columns of lace and tulle, he can always find an outlet in the --------- Club, a murky discotheque-bar, where, like so many multicoloured pots of jam, stroboscopic flashes are spattered over his clothes; and then, dazed and bewildered, stumble a hundred yards or so down the road to the London or Britannia, two popular pubs often resorted to by actors from the not-very-distant Playhouse Theatre. The last-named establishment, incidentally, is a great favourite among touring repertory companies and puts on a variety of shows, ranging from ballet, musicals, films, to farce and black comedy. A few years ago the theatre was partially burnt down. The fire, it is believed, was accidental and not an expression of protest by a member of the audience.

Allowing for facetiousness and exaggeration, this account does indicate something of Weston-super-Mare's quality; for it is a place, which, by relentlessly promoting money-consuming activities, creates and dictates the needs of its patrons. This is how you are to spend your earnings. It is an old formula, and it works.

Certainly, by night, the town goes all out to lure the visitor, and its

---

* The old penny 'What the Butler Saw' machines, with their grainy sepia tints and mildly erotic striptease sequences, have sadly passed on. The spinning rows of various fruits proffered by the one-armed bandits hardly compensate for the deep sense of bereavement felt by every sincere voyeur at their going.

illuminations compare favourably with those of Nice or Monaco. Fragile clusters of fairy lights, twinkling green, blue, red and orange, encircle the bay in an iridescent bracelet. Vivid neon squiggles flash their titles from the fronts of hotels, restaurants and clubs, and, lining the promenade, tall pearl-encased lamp-posts glimmer like giant matchsticks.

* * *

Regent Street is filled with amusement arcades and souvenir shops; it also has a flashy ornate neo-Classical cinema. Perhaps its best attraction is the Waxworks. They, at least, do exude atmosphere. The lower floor, depicting the usual miscellanea of individuals who have distinguished themselves in sport, showbiz, or, as is the case with royalty, by being merely born, is conventional enough, but the upper stage is especially appealing, being a claustrophobic gloomy chapel-like enclosure housing the less glittery celebrities. The present author, as a child, recalls many happy hours, alone in this darkly-lit chamber, browsing among the torture apparatus and exchanging stares with the mass murderers. More effectively set out than those of Madame Tussaud's, each criminal and instrument of pain is given an appropriate context: Dr Crippen, with little pebble-like spectacles, hovering over his victim in the bath; a man, eyes protruding to bursting-point, being slowly elongated; another about to be guillotined; another on the brink of disembowelment—a gallery of human cruelty.

Strolling along the promenade, it rapidly becomes evident that Weston is riddled with hotels. In and out of season, nearly all of the larger ones vigorously advertise their various commendatory features: cocktail lounges, free parking space, reduced terms for children, colour televisions, central heating, fitted razor plugs in all bedrooms, and other items of mechanical and electronic expertise that might come in useful to anyone desiring to animate a Frankenstein monster during their holiday. What even the most meagre and shabby of these boarding-houses used to advertise in the nineteenth century was—'Good Sea Views'. But there was often a catch in this innocent phrase. On more than one occasion, a puzzled holidaymaker, on being ushered into a drab basement room, would enquire the whereabouts of the breathtaking vista. The patient landlady would then tell him, that, if he were to take a five minute stroll down the road to the beach, the whole glorious prospect would unfold before his eyes and for no extra charge.

At the junction of Knightstone Road and Marine Parade is Leeves' Cottage. This fragment of antique Weston was built and occupied by the Rev. William Leeves. Former Guards' officer, this gentleman died in 1826 after being rector of Wrington for forty years. He is popularly credited with being the author of the popular song, 'Auld Robin Gray'—in actual fact, he wrote the music. Lady Anne Lindsay re-modelled the song from an early Scottish version. The ballad—a doleful slice of sentimental pie—concerns a young girl, Jenny, who, on the death of her sweetheart, finds herself unwillingly betrothed to Robin Gray, a 'gudeman' who safeguarded her family fortunes through difficult times. The couple are eventually married, and, soon afterwards, her young lover, Jamie, whom she had given up for drowned, returns and announces his decision to marry her. But now she feels compelled to reject him and resign herself to a life of perpetual remorse. The opening lines of the ballad, characteristically mournful and twilight-drenched, establish the right sort of atmosphere:

> When the sheep are in the fauld, and the kye come hame,
> When a' the weary warld to quiet rest are gane,
> The waes o' my heart fa' in showers frae my ee,
> Unkent to my gudeman wha sleeps sae sound by me.

The cynical may observe that 'gude auld Robin's' sleep was not unduly disturbed by the frantic convulsions of his wife's conscience.

Still running north Knightstone is eventually attained. Two hundred years ago this was a solitary rock and an island at high water. Its name was said to be derived from a Roman knight who had been stationed, either at the settlement at Uphill, or at the camp above, on the summit of Worlebury Hill. But such a belief can be attributed to a misunderstanding as to the earthwork's original occupiers. Some human bones of gigantic dimensions were discovered here when the rocks were being blasted for construction purposes. Today the Theatre and Warm Indoor Baths are sited on this promontory.

Passing the Marine Lake we approach Anchor Cove. This is an agreeable little creek with a narrow pebbly beach. In the days when mixed bathing was considered daring, or immoral, this spot was frequently resorted to by females and Peeping Toms were strongly discouraged. A rather witty footnote in Rutter's guide alludes to this matter:

> As the bathing place is appropriated exclusively to the ladies, gentlemen are considered as intruders, and will do well to avoid the indignation of the priestess of the retreat, though it may not prove as fatal as that of Diana to Actaeon.

* * *

Projecting 1,040 feet from the snout of Worlebury, the Birnbeck Pier houses the Lifeboat Station and was opened in 1869. Designed by Mr Birch, the pier is constructed of iron and has a steel jetty running at right angles to the main structure for 300 feet. In the summer months, the few remaining paddle steamers of the old White Funnel Fleet call, providing a service to Ilfracombe, Cardiff and Lundy Island. At one time the 'gull yellers' operated here—straining their vocal chords to the utmost lest the seagulls got their catch. In the past, this island, exposed as it is to the rapid ebb and flow of the tide, has proved a hazardous spot, the scene of at least one distressing incident:

> In the autumn of 1819, a melancholy and fatal accident occurred at this spot to the sons of C. A. Elton esq. They were amusing themselves in searching for small fish and shells on the rock, until their retreat was cut off

by the rapid rise of the tide, over the causeway. Not aware of the danger, they attempted to wade to the shore, but the youngest being carried away by the force of the current, the eldest rushed to rescue him, and both were swept away; the body of one was afterwards taken across to Newport, and that of the other to Clevedon.*

Nowadays Birnbeck Island is the headquarters of a sort of Victorian charade. The presiding genius of these genteel orgies is a gentleman who styles himself Lord Birnbeck. Guests are invited to join him, 'to wine and dine in the grand Victorian manner, enjoy the gay music hall entertainment and share in the general jollification'.

Not so many people are aware that the present Birnbeck Pier was not the first attempt to link the rocky outcrop with the mainland. A pier company attempted to make permanent the alliance by means of a bridge, but the bulldozing roarers of the Channel usurped this project, and, when the masonry was already far advanced, dashed it to mere component parts floating on the tide. So it all ended disastrously, but perhaps this is not quite the right word, for, by some inner perversity, human kind derives grim satisfaction from witnessing the destruction of fine ambitious projects: Fonthill tower abruptly collapsing, the brilliant wreckage of the Crystal Palace, Ozymandias, legless and eroded, surveying the surrounding desolation—that sort of thing, the puncturing and deflation of grandiosity. Anyhow someone had fun over the disappearance during a bad storm of Birnbeck's first pier. He was a poet of the Dundee school, who, possibly recalling the sparkling mediocrities of William Mc. Gonagall, wrote—

> Alas for the Pier! that wonderful Pier!
> 'Twas to bring the Westonians some thousands a-year:
> Ships, Schooners, and Brigs, all in multitude here
> Were to come from Japan, and South Wales, and Cape Clear,
> And steamers by dozens were soon to appear.

As for the Weston lifeboat, though it was probably less active than its Burnham counterpart, it was involved in a number of rescue operations, the outcome of which were not invariably joyous. During the hurricane of December 1900, the William James Holt, the second of Weston's boats, received a telegram from Captain Rowles, the pier master at Clevedon. He reported sighting two large ships aground on the Hook Sand. The William James was launched three-quarters of an hour later and swiftly made for the scene of the accident. When she reached the sands, it was already too late. One boat had sunk, the other was a wave-buckled wreck. The men had tried to save themselves by scrambling up the rigging, but the mainmast had snapped launching them into a violent grave. Later the boats were identified

---

* Their father, Charles Elton, dramatised the circumstances of their death in his poem, 'The Brothers', which contains a description of Clevedon Court. He was one of a talented group of literary men, including Lamb, Julius Hare, De Quincey and Barry Cornwall, who were regular contributors to the London Magazine. Elton achieved a solid reputation as a translator of the classical poets. He died at Bath in 1853.

as two Norwegian barques, the *Hovding* and *Tenax Propositi*. They were bound for South America with cargoes of coal.

* * *

Little is known of the beginnings of Weston-super-Mare. It is possible only to outline in generalised terms the various burial mounds, earthworks, hut circles and Roman villas, traces of all of which have been identified in the surrounding area. Detailed examination of this sort being outside the scope of the present volume, is necessary to recourse to the Domesday Book, a record, which, like a thin but penetrating beam of light, throws into sharp relief specific aspects of Feudal society.

Quoting from this massive work, most writers must feel a sense of inadequacy. To draw deductions about the 'villeins' and 'bordars' from the brisk statistics entered down is akin to trying to reconstruct a portrait of Thomas Hardy from his grocery list.

The peasants of Domesday are often portrayed by social historians as mere beasts of burden, their lives being on a similar level to the oxen they strapped to their ploughs. Money never worried them—they had none. Politics hardly affected them—their opinions were irrelevant. It was their lot only to work, which, from the age at which they learnt to toddle, to when, owing to fatigue, malnutrition and sickness they dropped dead, they did unceasingly.

Yet this view, conventionally stereotyped, is far from complete. What historians do not know is whether, despite the squalor and ceaseless toil, or even because of it, they were innerly invested with a capacity for exultation unknown in the twentieth century.

Because their lives were narrow and confined, the small indulgences they were granted on holidays and church festivals assumed a foremost significance. The labourer, on such occasions, could enjoy his share of hawking and hunting. He could visit the local pit where cock-fighting and bear-baiting sports would be staged. Or else there were archery and wrestling contests, stone-throwing competitions, and, in cold weather, skating on ice. Such pleasures broadened and enriched his existence.

Also, he had distinct legal rights. He could not be arbitrarily killed and maimed. If he died, his children were raised under the auspices of the manor to which he had been attached. His life, it is true, was fiercely restricted, but, in its own cramped and coded way, was reasonably secure.

Another factor was that he lived in a world where God and the Devil still radiated a chilling magnetic aura. Whether this gave his existence an extra dimension of awe and mystery, it is difficult to say. Historians, evading these points, stubbornly insist on drawing obvious contrasts between contemporary affluence and Feudal poverty. Wisely enough, they do not attempt to grapple with the psychological make-up of the Domesday worker, and they ever portray them as brutish shadowy figures, ploughing, tilling, carrying faggots, living with swine, sweating, digging, grinding, threshing—components in a remote and distant scheme.

Weston's Domesday status remains shadowy. A number of researchers, contrary to Collinson's view, doubt whether the parish figures as an independent entity in the record. Although a number of 'Westones' are included in the compilation, it is not always easy to pin-point their situation. In fact, it is the conviction of contemporary scholars that Weston-super-Mare at the period comprised part of the larger manor of Ashcombe. The Domesday entry for the latter read:

> Herluin holds from the Bishop (of Coutances) Aisecombe. Brictric held it in the time of King Edward, and paid Danegeld for three hides and a half. There is land for five plough-teams. In the demesne there are two plough-teams, and seven serfs and six villeins, and five boors with three plough-teams. There are forty acres of meadow, and three acres of coppice, and a hundred acres of pasture. It was and is worth a hundred shillings.

The 'Westone' quoted in the earlier histories was also held by the Bishop of Coutances. It seems, however, to have been a fairly modest holding, with seventeen acres of meadowland and enough arable to support three plough-teams. Its value was an unspectacular sixty shillings.

Later information, however, is distinct and verifiable. In the reign of Henry III, the manors of Weston and Ashcombe were held by William Arthur, Squire of Clapton Court. His descendants retained the holding until, by marriage, it passed to the Winter family. When Henry Winter died in 1685, Sir John Smyth, the family trustee, sold off the Weston estate along with other tenures. Samuel Gorge's son, Edward, according to an old book of parish accounts, owned the manor in 1694. He was the husband of Grace, the daughter of William Winter, so evidently the selling-off of the land had not been on an indiscriminate basis. Samuel Gorge was assigned the guardianship of Grace Winter after her father, William Winter, had been clapped in a Roundhead prison.

The next owner of the estate was John Pigott, esq., the descendants of whom were to play a vigorous role in the development of modern Weston. He acquired the manor in 1696.

* * *

A map of Weston-super-Mare, dated 1806, depicts a long and broad strip of beach going by the name of 'The Strand'; backing this, is an expanse called the 'Weston-super-Mare Moor' bisected by a thoroughfare called 'Watersill Road'. The village itself is a meagre sprinkling of dwellings strewn along a road called 'The Street'. It is noticeable that the community does not appear to have a strong local identity; all of the surrounding names are plain and nondescript. 'East Field', 'West Lane', 'Bristol Road'—names uncoloured by anecdote or regional idiosyncrasy.

Only sixteen years later the town had been 'discovered' as a resort, and a tidy little guidebook was produced, thin on factual matter, but elegantly written and printed by Chilcott's of Bristol. Weston, the booklet emphasises, is now a fashionable summer retreat renowned for the uncontaminated purity of its air.

In some ways it must have seemed a bleak and curious spot for a holiday.

Worlebury, at that time, was treeless, a smooth hippopotamus-back of a ridge, the grey stones of the earthwork strown like snow across its summit. The esplanade was not yet built. No pier linked Birnbeck Island with the mainland, and, only three years ago, the tragedy involving the Elton children had taken place.

Yet an impressive number of hotels had been established, including Fry's Hotel, the Plough, Bell Vue House, the Eagle House, and numerous other boarding-houses, many of which were situated among the sand-hills. A school for a hundred children had recently been erected, and, on the North Parade, was a seminary for 'Young Gentlemen' run by a Mr May, while 'Young Ladies', under the tuition of Mrs Downman, could attend an equally edifying institution at Wellington Place.

Health, not dissipation, the guide makes clear, was Weston's principal draw, and, apart from newspapers, billiards, pleasure boats and horse and cart rides, the amusements of the village were non-existent.

Only three bathing machines occupied the sands, but the hot and cold baths had already been erected at Knightstone: Another hot bath establishment in Somerset Place was presided over by Mrs Gill, a Boadicea of the waves, one of the 'original' bathing women of Weston. Those of a less aquatic turn of mind could enjoy the walks and scenic details of the area:

> From Claremont Lodge, the pedestrian may descend the hill by a winding path, and stroll among the rocks, which are formed into various romantic shapes; the tide rushing through the cavities produces an extraordinary sound; and, in one spot, forcing its way through a fissure in the rock, and then foaming over, it resembles a boiling kettle, which name it bears.

Yet, despite its limitations amenity-wise, people seemed to have enjoyed Weston to the fullest. On clear sunny evenings the sands would be crowded. Everywhere there would be the steady clop of hooves and the rapid click of revolving axles as horses, ponies, donkeys, carriages, sedan and wheel chairs, careered back and forth along the beach. Others would simply stroll, hatted, in groups, engrossed in conversation; others would be seated, listening to music or smoking; and there would be others who would gaze across the bay, far into the evening, until the sky inked over, and the sun—a flaming gash on the darkening blue—finally slotted into the horizon and only the steady flash of the Flatholm light, the stars and the distant glitter of Newport and Cardiff attracted attention.

* * *

The encampment of Worlebury Hill (first century B.C.) rises gently above Weston. Tall Victorian villas, like massive grey whelks, cling resolutely to its slopes. At one time it was bare, craggy and shorn of vegetation, but Smyth Pigott, the contemporary lord of the manor, after planting oak and larch, opened it up to the public in the early half of the nineteenth century. The path running up through the woods from the south penetrates a maze of pits and scattered masonry. The former have been interpreted both as dwelling-places and as grain-storage repositories.

The fortifications are extensive. Two ramparts, about fifteen feet high and composed entirely of stones, cross the hill and continue westwards enclosing an area of some ten acres. The northern scarp face of the hill, falling away sharply to the Channel, adequately defended itself and was penetrated by a large cave—now blocked with stones—leading to the summit.

The history of the fort, like its foundations, is multi-layered and complex: a microcosm of the history of early Britain. It bears traces of both Iron and Bronze Age occupation and coins of the Roman Empire have also been uncovered. Its name appears in the Anglo-Saxon Chronicle. Apparently, in the reign of Alfred, the Danes, after being repelled by native forces, sought refuge on the hill. When they left the encampment and advanced to Biddisham, they were completely routed and their headquarters at Worlebury subsequently taken and burnt.

Near the point on the hill where a maze of footpaths intersect is a loose heap of stones known as the Peak Winnard. C. W. Dymond, the archaeologist, determined to probe the secrets of this mysterious pile, removed these and proceeded to dig the soil underneath. His efforts were crowned by the discovery of two bits of bone and three limpet shells.

A superstition of sorts is connected with this cairn. Fishermen, crossing the hill to their nets at Birnbeck, were alleged to casually add a stone to the mound and chant:

> Picwinner, Picwinner!
> Pick me some dinner!

There may, for all I know, be some hidden significance in this futile practice. If so, it eludes me.

If the Peak Winnard cairn revealed nothing exciting, other sites on Worlebury Hill have yielded invaluable archaeological material. Excavations have revealed that, at various periods, the camp has been ravaged by both the fire and the sword. Three skeletons were found in one of the pits, piled on top of each other, as if they had fallen in whilst engaged in combat. One had a great cleft in his skull; another had his collar bone rammed up his jaw and a huge pebble embedded in his skull; a third had an iron spearhead protruding from his spine. These grisly souvenirs, safely emtombed in glass, are now giggled over by parties of schoolchildren and sundry browsers at Taunton Museum.

* * *

A less-documented aspect of Worlebury are its deserted lead and calamine workings. First identified by German mineralogists in the reign of Elizabeth, the deposits scored the limestone in veins following the general east-west strike of the hill. The principal use of the ore was in brass-making, for calamine, if combined with copper, produces this rust-resistant alloy. Worlebury calamine was held to be of exceptionally high quality and was supplied to the brass-making works at Tintern. A similar factory was not established in Bristol until as late as 1702. Later when it was discovered that spelter—a commercial zinc employed in making ornaments—could be extracted from calamine, the industry enjoyed another boom, but by the middle years of the nineteenth century the taxes had been dropped on the cheap foreign ores imported into the country, and Mendip and Worlebury calamine ceased to be competitive. The lead sulphide, galena—a soft grey mineral—was worked alongside the calamine in less appreciable quantities. Remnants of Worlebury's mining industry may be seen on the north side of the hill. Dotted here and there, below the encampment, along the Old Pier Road, are blocked-up shafts and shallow weed-filled pits: mouldering debris of burrowing bipeds.

UPHILL, BLEADON, LYMPSHAM AND BRENT KNOLL

CLINGING to the skirts of an incline which is really an offshoot of Bleadon, Uphill—spelt 'Opophille' in the Domesday Book—is a name of Danish or Frisian origin and means 'Hubba's Pill' or harbour. Hubba, who captained a ship, enlivened these shores with his exploits in the ninth century. There is a story that Edmund, King and Martyr, was taken captive by this vigorous gentleman and offered his freedom, only on the condition that he renounced his Christian faith. Edmund declined to do this. Hubba promptly lashed him to an oak tree and fired a bolt through his heart, and it is alleged that this actual projectile now resides in the British Museum. Like most people who live dangerously, Hubba himself was killed—in battle against Alfred the Great, but his banner still flutters proudly and is borne by all those with the name Hobbs in Somerset.

The town was once important as a Roman port and station. A road ends here; formerly it was linked with Charterhouse on the Mendips and Old Sarum in Wiltshire. Lead and tin were shipped down the Axe and on to foreign ports. Today is is nondescript hotpotch of old and new. The Castle—an imposing building with a turreted porch—has a fine situation; otherwise, apart from some pleasant ivy-clad farmhouses and a fine old bridge, there is only the ruined church. Perched precariously as any chamois on the lip of a sheer cliff, this building combines Norman and later styles. At one time the tower was whitewashed and used by sailors as a landmark; on its south side there is a malignant three-faced gargoyle. The site of the church is on the Roman station, Ad Axium, and many coins have been found here. The last official service was in April 1846.

The general aspect of this small anchorage, with its hilltop church and raw sabre-faced cliff, is a little unusual. Small wonder that extraordinary geophysical phenomena have occurred here. For instance, it is recorded in

'Brittania Baconia', published in 1661, that the ground here was suffering from a cyst or boil of sorts. Apparently it gradually swelled up, and, after a brief period of ripening, collapsed in a spectacular manner. The exact entry runs:

> It is reported that about Uphill (a parish by the sea-side not far from Axbridge) within these half-hundred years, a parcel of ground swelled up like a hill, and on a sudden clave asunder, and fell down again into the earth, and in place of it remains a great pool.

While the growth of the hill would be difficult to account for, the sudden disappearance which left behind a water-filled depression is by no means unknown. In limestone regions, where the rock is being permanently eaten and dissolved by rainfall, highly developed cave-systems often fall-in and leave basins where water may accumulate.

Uphill Castle is a morbid-looking Tudor fantasia. George Bennett puts its date around 1805, later additions to it being made in 1828, but certainly, apart from its year of origin, it is a very un-Regency structure. Hollywood, filming the 'Knights of the Round Table', would erect such backdrops—although the Victorian conservatory would obtrude. Set in spacious, well-wooded grounds, bristling with flowers and shrubs, it is less ostentatious than its Banwell counterpart, but creates a similar impression of copycat romanticism: crenellations, parapets, mullioned windows and a turretted porch, one can easily imagine Mr Thomas Tutton Knyfton, who was responsible for its more exotic architectural garnishings, pointing to an illustration of a castle in his copy of 'Ivanhoe' and saying to the architect—'Could you make my house look like this please?'

Once Uphill flourished in a modest sort of way as a port, taking in coal and iron from South Wales, exporting local dairy produce. The Hobb's Boat Inn, on the Bleadon Road, is a relic of those days, being formerly the principal ferrying point of the Axe. Lympsham and Bleadon, too, were pint-sized harbours, dispatching coal from Lydney, potatoes and sand. The last boat to call was the *Democrat* in 1942.

Much earlier, the village figured in an act of flagrant piracy. In 1591, the *Gray honde*, a French merchant ship, was captured in the Atlantic and taken into Uphill Harbour. It had been returning from Newfoundland to Bayonne and was carrying 'one houndred and eight thousand of drye fishes, and fowre thousand of greene fishes, and fowre-tenne hogsheades of trayne oyles.' The warship which had impounded it belonged to none other than that highly civilised poeticising adventurer, Sir Walter Raleigh, who, no doubt, enjoyed a fair share of the 'six thousand crownes' of bounty. Peter de Hody, the French merchant who owned the Greyhound, was anxious to claim damages for this considerable injustice. He sent two envoys to England to make enquiries. Predictably their reception was brutal and intimidatory:

> So as havinge spent v. crownes, they were fayne to leave of their sute, and to returne homwardes into Fraunce, for to save their lyfes, beinge every daie threatned by the owners and victellers of the said shippe of war, who

being riche marchauntes of Bristoll, have receyved the procedinges of the said marchandises, and with holde still the said shippe in their Custody.

* * *

The main A370 road passes by the Manor Farm at Uphill and touches the outskirts of Bleadon. This town, built on the slope of a hill of the same name, is believed to derive its name from 'bleak-down', or 'bleo', 'blow', the 'windy down'. It has, however, been more crudely translated as evolving from 'bleeding'—that epithet much beloved by Cockney scriptwriters—as the place where a gory and decisive battle was fought against the Danes.

The heroine of this skirmish, incidentally, was an old woman, who, by cutting the cables of the longships, blocked off their retreat and injected fresh spunk into the local lads. They dealt death among the flaxen-haired delinquents with every blow of their antique farming implements.

The church of SS Peter and Paul, dedicated in 1317, has a fine tower which was struck by lightning in 1832. A pinnacle at the south-west corner of the fabric was thrown down and several stones on the west face were ejected—'The lightning travelled as far as the village smithy, the roof of which it broke, and stretched the blacksmith for some time insensible beside his forge.'

In 1053 it is recorded that the church belonged to Gytha, the mother of Harold Godwin, who, after the failure of the Exeter insurrection, sought refuge on Steepholm. She conferred the advowson of the church, together with that of the manor, upon the cathedral at Winchester. The chancel houses two unusual effigies known locally as 'Adam and Eve'; in the churchyard is an ancient stone cross with a fluted, tapering shaft, and a stepped base.

A century ago, the rector of Bleadon was the Rev. C. D. Russell, geologist, character, and lover of the Mendip Hills. Perhaps more than anyone else, he devoted his life to elucidating their stratigraphical and mineralogical secrets. His reputation extended beyond Somerset, for an article was devoted to him in the London Magazine, a quite different affair, in those days, from the modish *avante garde* periodical that comes out every two months now.

His home, the writer recorded, was crammed with rocks. They occupied sofas, chairs, tables—even the lawn and the approaches to the building were strown with fossils. As for the Old Man of the Mendips himself—'In the midst of a large room, densely tenanted, sat the geologist, as on a narrow isthmus, between the labours of the past and the triumphs of the future; like Marius amidst the ruins of Carthage, or (if you will) like a half-tide rock in a mountain sea.'

The Western Railway passes through a cutting dividing Bleadon and Uphill. While this was being excavated, a strike arose among the navvies who were dissatisfied with their wages. Brunel was supervising the work at the time, but his august presence did not pacify the disgruntled working force. He sent for Mr Knyfton, of Uphill Castle, who was the local magistrate. The latter, in due course, appeared with a copy of the Riot Act. Boldly, he strode among the jeers and dungarees, exhorting them to conduct themselves with dignity and restraint, telling them that, if they chose to ignore his counsel, the gallant cavalrymen from Horfield Barracks would forcefully restore them to order. The men were clearly impressed by this performance. He returned to his comfortable and stately mansion, they to their picks and shovels.

* * *

In and around Bleadon there is little notable architecture, but there are some buildings of slightly more than passing interest. East of the village, for instance, are a group of houses called Wonderstone. They are remarkable for their stonework consisting of yellow translucent crystals of carbonate of lime in an earthy-red dolomite matrix. Shiplate House, not far from Loxton, is a tasteful eighteenth-century edifice of two storeys. It is solidly constructed out of red brick with stone facings. A more opulent residence, the Webbington Country Club, lies beneath the shadow of Crook's Peak. This large timbered mansion, with its swanky pretensions and Tudor gables, was built in 1907 and advertises itself as the 'Nitespot' of the West. Entertainment takes various forms here: women relinquishing articles of clothing to raucous whistles of encouragement, simulated black magic rituals to gasps of morbid curiosity, stand up comic turns to the clamouring guffaws of the initiated and the blank bewildered stares of the pure in heart and mind.

Moving south the A370 passes Lympsham. This village was virtually rebuilt by its local squire over a hundred years ago, and the prevailing architectural movement of the time is reflected in the lancet-headed windows of the cottage dwellings.

Curiously enough, till now, most books on Somerset have virtually ignored this attractive hamlet. Even the pedantic and thorough Reverend Collinson, excluding his description of the parish church, produced a summary in the 1790s which amounted to little more than a house-counting exercise:

> The parish contains fifty houses, and about three hundred and twenty inhabitants. About forty of the houses stand near the church, of the rest fifteen are in the hamlet of Edingworth, sometimes called Endeston, thence Eastward-Town, and thence by corruption Easterton, nearly a mile to the east, part of which belongs to East Brent; and three are in the small hamlet called Batch, in the road to Uphill.

John Rutter, forty years later, repeated this performance, then remarked briefly on the increased population which he attributed to the village's 'salubruity' and vastly improved drainage scheme.

But both of these antiquarians can be excused this oversight: Collinson wrote his survey before the construction of the ornate manor house, and Rutter at a time when the very newness of the architecture was from his viewpoint a disqualification in itself.

Today, the hamlet is a pleasing museum of Gothic Revivalism: spires, sham battlements, long thin windows with plate tracery, trefoiled panels, crocketed pinnacles—all the familiar accoutrements of a much-maligned architectural fashion.

The Manor House, formerly the Rectory, has pride of place among such exhibits. Set in landscaped grounds with a small lake, it is a very fancy, orchidaceous affair, almost Rococo, with its dazzling white battlements, polygonal towers and simulated Tudor bay windows. Rutter, possibly regarding it as an error of taste, paid a tribute to the well-kept lawns encircling the edifice and the kindly co-operation of the Reverend Stephenson in loaning his print for inclusion in his own valuable work, but refrained from commenting on the abode's artistic merits or lack of them.

Yet now, mellowed a little, the building is undoubtedly effective. Current attitudes are more kindly disposed towards nineteenth-century Gothicism. John Betjeman, in particular, championed this muddled and often morbid style, and the manor house, although of a pre-Victorian date, embodies many of the faults and virtues inherent in later structures.

If its lines are not strong and harmonious, they do have a lively variety, and the view of the gleaming chalky battlements from the back of the house, rising magically above a liquid mirror and fluttering penants of emerald foliage, is as fine as any in North Somerset.

In the garden of the manor is an inscribed pinnacle. A similar obelisk is situated nearby in the village, decorated with trefoils at its base and bearing the following irreproachable sentiments: Fear God. Honour the King. Love one another.

Other buildings include the Manor Hall, erected at the cost of £1,800 by Rev. J. H. Stephenson, as a memorial to his father. The structure, drab and ugly, is of limestone with Bath stone facings.

The fifteenth-century parish church of Saint Christopher has a wagon-roof in the nave and some richly-panelled ceilings. It also—like many local barflies, has a propensity to lean.

> Dearer to me thine ancient steeple grey
> Raised by some pious hand some bygone day
> With massy buttresses and niches fair,
> And towering pinnacles that pierce the air
> Than e'en proud Salisbury's spire, amazing height,
> Which rises upward four times the height.

These lines were penned by the Reverend Joseph Henry Stephenson, the laureate of Lympsham, when he was a lad of seventeen. The facile bathos of the last line indicates the rather pale quality of the majority of his verses. Despite this, they were printed regularly in local journals and a collected edition of them, published by the Athenaeum Press of Taunton, appeared in 1898. As a Treasurer and Prebendary of Wells Cathedral, he was an influential and well-thought-of cleric. If his poems are not literary landmines, they do breathe an English quality of mild pastoral sweetness. Notably he was a very patriotic bard. Allusions to Brent Knoll, Bleadon church tower, the Mendips, Uphill's 'bleak and barren height', and various other local topographical paraphernalia recur in his works. He also wrote affectionately of 'old Crook':

> Bordered beneath by emerald plain,
> Wide stretching westward to the main,

> Thou flinty peak arise:
> And with thy kindred heights around,
> Scorn trees and towers on humbler ground,
> And lift thee to the skies!
>
> Bleak desolation yonder reigns,
> As turn we from the southern plains,
> Where sunbeams glow and smile:
> And far 'mid Mendip's forest lone
> We gaze o'er sedge and 'cold grey zone'
> For many a dreary mile.

The name Lympsham still poses something of an enigma. A plausible explanation links its first syllable with places like Lyme Regis or Limpley Stoke, towns standing near boundary or limitary lines of some sort. J. S. Hill, in his erudite study of Somerset personal and placenames, forwarded the engaging suggestion that 'Lympsham' may have some connection with 'Lumpel'—a German word meaning ragamuffin. This, of course, has no reflection upon the amiable inhabitants of the village.

* * *

Conspicuous around these parts is the monadnock of Brent Knoll. An old story goes that the Devil, while he was busy digging out Cheddar Gorge, threw down a spadeful of earth and thus created the landmark. Geologically an outlier of the Mendips, this flat-topped hill looms above the plain, like a squashed clown's hat. On its summit is the remains of an Iron Age encampment, and clinging to its slopes are the villages of Brent Knoll and East Brent.

The former has an interesting church, the inner doorway of which dates from the twelfth century. Dedicated to Saint Michael, one of its most individual features are the carved bench-ends illustrating the legend of an abbot-fox who attempted to despoil the secular clergy of Brent. This antique comic strip attracted the attention of Sir Nikolaus Pevsner:

> On the first Reynard the Fox is seen disguised as a mitred abbot. He is paid respects to by three monks in cowls who have the heads of swine. On the

Brent Knoll

second the fox is foot-cuffed and put below into the stocks, and the monkeys guard him. His mitre hangs on the wall. On the third he is hung by the triumphant geese. What does this imply? A general hatred of the parishoners or some wealthy donor for monasteries and Glastonbury in particular? Or a topical reference which escapes us?

The explanation is, as a matter of fact, fairly straightforward. The benchends, so it would appear, tell a tale of triumph. The fox represents a covetous Glastonbury abbot, the geese are the parishioners of Brent, and the dogs stand for the two churchwardens. The abbot, in the same way as a fox preys upon geese, tries to appropriate the rich revenues of Brent, but is foiled in the process. He ends up in the stocks, and, finally, on the gallows—jeered-at and executed by his own flock. There is savagery and mockery in this angry little squib.

Also within the fabric is the altar tomb to John Somerset and his two wives—a mural monument which C. G. Harper described with exuberant facetiousness:

> John Somerset himself is represented in half length, with a portrait-bust of a wife on either side. There are, further, effigies of himself and the two Mrs Somerset praying, accompanied by a chrissom child; together with an alarming effigy starting up in a coffin and praying earnestly to an angel who, armed with a trumpet like a megaphone, wallows amid clouds which issue from the trumpet visibly in lengths, not unlike news from modern tape machines. An elderly angel, with an oily smile of smug satisfaction, beams greasily below.

A modern nativity play—'The Business of Good Government'—received its first performance in St Michael's. Its author, John Arden, re-interpreted the role of Herod in a lively and provocative fashion, and there were moments when the writing soared to lyricism. The cast was drawn from local people.

A track from the church leads to the Manor House. Lying high and dry on the slopes of the knoll, this building was designed by John Norton, the architect responsible for the Gothic virtuosities of Tyntesfield. It was erected over the period 1862–64.

* * *

Like Brent Knoll, East Brent is a dispersed settlement. Comprising a pub, two churches, numerous farms and cottages, it is a hamlet one is barely aware of as one passes through it. Orchards dot the slopes of the knoll on this side, and springs emerge where the water meets layers of impermeable shale. Terracing is noticeable on the hill slopes. The softer clays have been eroded and the harder bands of rock have formed these shelves.

In the Domesday Record, East Brent figures as 'Brentmerse' (Brent Marsh), and, like South Brent and Lympsham, it was owned for centuries by the prosperous abbey of Glastonbury. Predictably, it was not valued all that highly; in 1293, along with the other two parishes and Berrow, its total value was only estimated at £130 4s.

Once an important manor house stood here. Built by Abbot Selwood in the fifteenth century, it was appointed with fine 'guesten' chambers and was destroyed in 1708.* A group of trees compensate for its absence today.

The parish church, St Mary's, in the Transitional style, has marked claims to distinction. Pevsner singled out its spire as one of the most elegant in Somerset. The interior has an organ gallery dated 1635, a Jacobean pulpit, and an east window depicting the 'Passion and Ascension of Our Lord' and the 'Coronation of the Virgin'.

The word 'Brent' has undergone the usual multiplicity of interpretations, and, among other translations, is said to be derived from 'Burnt Knoll', a hilltop site where beacons were lighted; alternatively, the scene of violent routing by fire. Then it might be a corruption of 'Brien', or 'Brenne', 'Bryan', the family name of former lords of the manor of Brean. Failing this, there is always the Scandinavian word 'Brant', or 'Brand', meaning a steep slope.

* * *

As one moves southwards from Brent, it is noticeable how the shape of the Knoll changes. Its lumpy uneven outline assumes a more forceful symmetry until, from viewpoints outside Highbridge and other spots, it resembles a cone. Like Crook's Peak, it has been described by locals as the stump of an ancient volcano, a statement which is geological nonsense. Nevertheless, this distinctive uplift, like Glastonbury Tor, does succeed in dominating the country for many miles around, and, in the blue-grey muddy light, swimming above the misty flats, emanates a similar aura of mystery. The historian, William of Malmesbury, recorded that it was once known as 'Mons Ranarum'—the mountain of frogs; and John Rutter, in his account, although he greatly exaggerates the outlier's height, communicates its archaeological significance:

> The hill is more than a thousand feet above the level of the sea, and is crowned by a large, double irregular entrenchment, in which brass and silver coins of the Roman Empire have been frequently found; and by digging at its base, heads of weapons, fibulae, urns, and other remains, have been thrown up, most probably from the sites of numerous barrows and tumuli, which were once scattered over the low land, or flats, even as far as Cheddar Hill, until agriculture had worn them down to a level with the surrounding ground.

* * *

---

* It belonged to the Abbey of Glastonbury and was used as a residence or boarding-house for monks.

THE TOTTS
(BREAN TO BERROW)

FROM the sea-front at Weston, the promontory of Brean Down* can be clearly identified. Its sleek and sinister outline, like a surfacing Loch Ness Monster, dominates the southern end of the bay. Extending 1½ miles into the Bristol Channel, this whalebacked peninsula is treeless and exposed; on its southern side grassy cliffs rise to over 300 feet. Rare plants, such as the White Rock Rose, flower here from May to July, and whelks, limpets, sea-snails and other shell fish are found on the rocks. Rock Samphire is also common. The country folk once pickled it and sold it inland. Of outstanding interest is the bird life: three species, in particular, are closely-guarded on the Down.

> Every year for 50 years at least a pair of ravens had their eyrie in the cliffs on the southern side, and it is not uncommon in the spring to see five ravens there together. A nobler and more beautiful figure than the raven is the peregrine falcon, which, driven away by persecution from its ancient haunt on Steep Holme, has lately established itself in the cliffs of Brean Down. The third species specially protected is that most beautiful of all our native waterfowl, the sheldrake, otherwise called, from its habit of laying eggs in a hole, often a rabbit-hole, the burrow-duck, most conspicuously dressed in white and brown and chestnut and with dark green and glossy head and neck.†

The Down also has a varied history. The Phoenicians are said to have traded here with the Ancient Britons, probably for lead and tin from the Mendips, and it is also cited as one of the points of departure of the Roman legions. In 1866, anticipating an invasion from Napoleon, the Down was fortified:

* The name is derived from *Bryn*, British for 'hill', and was later transferred to the lords of the manor—Brene or Brien.

† *The Times*,———, 1912.

66

Brean Down On the north side of the parish is Brean Down, a high peninsula extending near a mile into the channel in a north-west direction. (Collinson)

7-inch canons were mounted on the hilltop, and buildings were erected to house 30 men and 20 horses. But, in July 1900, an enterprising soldier fired his rifle into the powder magazine and eliminated himself and the defence installations. The fort was later dismantled and re-occupied during the world wars.

It is odd to think that the Down was very nearly a major Atlantic port. As early as 1841, Captain Evans, who later rose to the rank of Admiral, was extolling its advantages as a potential deep-sea harbour to a Select Committee of the House of Commons. Some twenty years later, the 'Brean Down Harbour and Railway Act' went officially through Parliament, and the newly-formed company started scavenging for shareholders and wealthy patrons. Among other enticements, this is how the company presented the Down's case against those of the major English ports:

> Brean Down occupies the finest situation in the country for a Trans-Atlantic Port... The track for vessels being in direct line to New York would avoid the circuitous and sometimes dangerous detour by the Irish Channel, and the serious delay often caused by the bar at the mouth of the River Mersey... The saving in time by the Brean Down route between America and London would be nearly one whole day... The distance from London to Brean Down is only 140 miles compared with 200 miles from Liverpool to London...

In 1864, Lady Wilmot laid the first stone of the harbour and work got underway. The party afterwards retired to the Town Hall at Weston-super-Mare where a large champagne luncheon had been prepared. While this was in progress, the foundation stone, to which was attached a gaily-painted buoy and a small flag embroidered with the initials B. D. H., was sighted floating down the Channel. Someone had seriously underestimated the capabilities of the local tides.

This ominous omen proved prophetic. The Brean Harbour Scheme, owing to constructional and financial difficulties made little progress. A vast sum was lavished on the erection of a pier, the corroded foundations of which may still be observed at low water. The great storm of 1872 accounted for the rest. Some of the earliest experiments in wireless telegraphy were conducted by

Marconi on the Down. The very first message, transmitted by him from Lavernock in South Wales, was picked up here in May 1896.

Today a stroll over the Down still counts as an enjoyable experience. There is a tarred road, dating from the foundation of the fort, running almost the entire length of the promontory. On the southern side of the uplift, not far from the Bronze Age Burial Barrow, are the overgrown foundations of a Roman Temple. From time to time, industrious moles excavate pottery of that date, and for war addicts, there are bases of nissen huts and anti-tank and aircraft guns.

The Brean and Weston area, ever-wary of Gallic visitors, has a long record of batteries and armaments. As early as 1872, a writer in the Weston-super-Mare Gazette reported that Flatholm sustained a 'fine force' of Royal Artillery men, 51 strong. The newsman, with childish awe, goes on to say that the 'terrible' Moncrieff guns are being installed on the island's batteries. These fearful 'engines of destruction', of 7-inch calibre, weighed seven tons and were capable of hurling a 2-cwt projectile an 'amazing' distance. In fairness to this timorous soul, it must be admitted that photographs of these weapons do bear out his description. They do, indeed, look gaunt and brutal blocks of machinery, as they lie, sleek and oiled, in huge circular pits, their iron barrels protruding like black candles of death.

In 1892, Staff Surgeon Rahilly of the Army Medical Department, submitted the following details relating to the Severn Defences: *Garrisons*—The forts, Brean Down, Steep and Flat Holm, are garrisoned by detachments of the Coast Brigade Royal Artillery. At present the strength is—Gunners: Brean Down, 5; Steep Holm, 5; Flat Holm, 5. *Barracks*—The barracks are built on the latest and most approved hygienic principles, and afford ample cubic and superficial space for the following number of men: Brean Down, 21; Steep Holm, 28; Flat Holm, 29; to which strength the garrison can be raised, if necessary, in a few hours. *Armaments*—Brean Down—The fort faces north, and numbers seven 7-inch 7-ton muzzle-loading rifled guns in position. Birnbeck Island being 4,450 yards; Steep Holm, 5,200 yards; and Flat Holm, 8,400 yards distant. *Steep Holm*—The battery is 250 feet above sea level, mounting nine 7-inch 7-ton muzzle-loading guns on the summit of the island, in such positions as to effectually command the channel between it and Brean Down and Flat Holm. *Flat Holm* has ten 7-inch 7-ton muzzle-loading rifled guns in battery, at an elevation of 130 feet above sea level. These forts, which were open to visitors on application to the master gunners in charge, completed, with Fort Lavernock on the Welsh coast, the chain of defences protecting the mouth of the Severn.

* * *

The village of Brean, lying near the estuary of the River Axe, is five miles north of Burnham. In 1607, according to a contemporary pamphlet, it suffered severe losses from flooding:

> 'The parish of Breane is swallowed (for the most part) up by the waters. In it stood but nine houses, and of those seaven were consumed, and with XXVI persons lost their lives.'

Keeping the sea at bay had evidently posed a problem here for some time. An ancient deed states that Thomas Baret, bishop of Knachdune in Ireland, and a suffragan bishop of Bath and Wells, in 1484—'hath a moytie of the lordship of Brean in Brent Marsh, so long as he shall stand a personal surety there, so that he, with the revenue, fortifie the sea walls and banks for the salvation of the said lordship'.

The parish church of Saint Bridget, in the Later Perpendicular style, has a stunted tower crowned by a saddleback roof: lightning destroyed its upper section in 1729. The church was restored in 1883, the chancel being rebuilt, the old pebble floor re-paved, and a reredos of Dumfries stone installed. The dedication, to a popular Irish saint, is unusual this far east. Born at Faugher, near Dundalk in Ulster, Bridget was a sweet and industrious woman who bettered the condition of ailing sheep, tended the blind, fed the poor, converted the mad to Christ, and was held out as 'a marvellous ladder for pagans to visit the kingdom of Mary's son'. She died at Kildare on February 1st, A.D. 523.

Inside the building is an eagle lectern, erected in memory of W. Sperring esq., who was for 47 years churchwarden. A stone figure of a soldier commemorates those who lost their lives in the Great War and stands in the churchyard.

Francis Knight, in his admirably-documented study, 'The Sea-Board of Mendip', records that Brean village in 1902 was still sufficiently cut-off and isolated from the world to retain its own idiosyncratic remedies for familiar ailments. One of them involved the use of spiders to manufacture a pill to relieve ague. The insect was crushed and rolled up in a pellet of bread—and swallowed. In summer, sandwiches may be bought at reasonable prices in the stalls and kiosks around the sands.

Knight also refers to an old book of accounts containing some novel approaches to veterinary science. For instance, to cure a sick cow, it recommends that three live eels should be thrust down its throat—a measure which, if it did not remedy the beast's malady, was guaranteed to make it shift.

* * *

Dune country proper starts at Brean, a monotonous landscape of sandy dips and scarps, the movements of which are minutely recorded by scientific bodies. Surface drainage is negligible, most water seeping underneath or being absorbed by sand.

It is not a prepossessing terrain in any way, but it has a certain dreary charm all its own. The sky is usually the colour of chalky water, with bars of bluish vapour stretching across the horizon; inland, it is all green, the blurred lifeless green of weeds stagnating at the bottom of a pond. When the wind blows fiercely, long eel-like whips of sand twist across the beach and hiss viperously.

Everywhere there is a look of scragginess. Like a half-shaved beard, the dunes are in places unmarked; elsewhere rife with coarse vegetation, car parks, squat bungalows and caravan sites.

Even if the place does remind one of a clapboard holiday desert, its climate—though moist and blowy—compares well with other parts. Short, mild winters are one of the attractions of this part of the country, especially to the elderly and retired, for the climate of the coastal belt, while eschewing any Polynesian allurements of hot sunshine and scented breezes, is tolerable and temperate. The most important months for sunshine are May, June and July, the average duration of it in the year being around 1,600 hours. As far as precipitation is concerned, the area is akin to that of the Midlands or Southern and Central England. There is a measurable rainshadow effect, lessening eastwards from Exmoor to the Somerset Plain, ensuring that the region does not experience the more turbulent weather of the Devon and Cornwall peninsula.

The climate, however, over the past thousand years, has witnessed some fairly dramatic changes, and it is with a jolt one reads in the Domesday Book that Edward the Confessor made a gift to the Abbey of Glastonbury of a modest tenure called 'Padeneberie'. Lying in the parish of Wedmore, what was significant about this small estate was that it supported vineyards—'Another island belonging thereto is called Padeneberie. There are six acres of arable land, and three arpents of vineyard, and one bordarius; it is worth four shillings.' Today this hamlet is called Pamborough.

* * *

Walking over the 'Totts' one is liable to become aware of the sizeable rabbit population. Sometimes, as if catapulted by some unseen force, they shoot out of a hedge and thump and scurry across the sandy turf. It is the appetites of these furry cannonballs, combined with their legendary proliferation, which maintains the tidy close-cropped swathes of grass on the Down, and their hairs in fox droppings testify to the manner in which they occasionally come to grief. In former times, far from being considered as material for Beatrix Potter or the originals of those beribboned jujus that dangle from windscreens, their presence on tracts of wasteland was counted as a solid asset. There is a deed, dated 34th of Edward III, 1360, wherein Robert Brene, lord of certain parcels of Brene in Brent Marsh, grants to Sir Thomas Hege 'all his rabbits in the parcel of Brene Down'—magnanimity indeed!

Another visitor is Brock the Badger. Being mainly nocturnal, he is seldom seen, but strolling across the dunes on a moonlit evening, one may be privileged enough to catch a glimpse of his dusky form noiselessly breaching a gap in a hedgerow or stealing along the edge of the slacks. Feeding on roots, delicacies such as bluebell bulbs, insects, fruit and young rabbits in spring, the only daylight traces of him are paw marks in the sand or mud. Among other residents in these parts can be numbered weasels, field mice, voles and shrews.

* * *

The bladderwrack which accumulates along the Brean shoreline is fairly impressive: fragments of ships' planking, cups, glass, pottery and

Worle. The Observatory.
Formerly it was a windmill.

War Memorial stands in
main shopping centre.

Worle Church. The South Door exhibits
some early 12th century work.

Kenn. The Parish Church.

Kewstoke. The Monk's Steps, August

Weston-super-Mare. Royal Crescent.

Weston-super-Mare. The Town Hall.

Weston-super-M
Birnbeck Pier.

on-super-Mare. Statue of 'Vanity'
entrance to Winter Gardens.

on-super-Mare. The Bandstand in
e Park, with the tower of St. John's
ging from the trees to the left.

on-super-Mare.
Reverend Leeves' Cottage.

above: Weston-super-Mare. Constitutional Club.
below: Weston-super-Mare. Oriel Terrace.

Worlebury Woo[d]
The 'Peak Wina[?]
cairn. Allegedly [the]
work of fisherme[n]
—although 'Wi[ne]
was a 7th Centu[ry]
Bishop of Wesse[x]

Worlebury Camp,
Weston-super-Mare.
Pottery and bronze
implements unearthed
here suggest that the
fortress was stormed
by the Romans while
occupied by the
Belgae in the 1st
Century A.D.

Pit-dwelling,
Worlebury Cam[p]
Weston-super-M[are]
These large pits,
into the limesto[ne]
to a depth of ab[out]
seven feet, have [been]
identified both a[s]
crude homestead[s of]
the first settlers [on the]
hill and as grana[ries]
or rubbish-pits. [The]
latter of these tw[o]
explanations ha[s]
been popularly
adopted.

lebury Woods. These woods, replete
ash, beech, alder, sycamore, yew, oak
Scots Pine, were first planted by
th-Pigott in 1823.

Weston-super-Mare. An example of architectural bric-a-brac in which Weston abounds.

ston-super-Mare. The Cemetery.

Lympsham. The Parish Church.

The Old Railway Wharf, the Yeo Estuary, November 1974.

The Iron Railway Bridge, the Yeo Estuary, November 1974.

Uphill Castle.

Uphill. This cliff-face is a favourite retreat of geologists. The bedded limestone is distinctly exposed.

...mpsham. The ...nor House—as ...ved from the rear.

Lympsham. The School House.

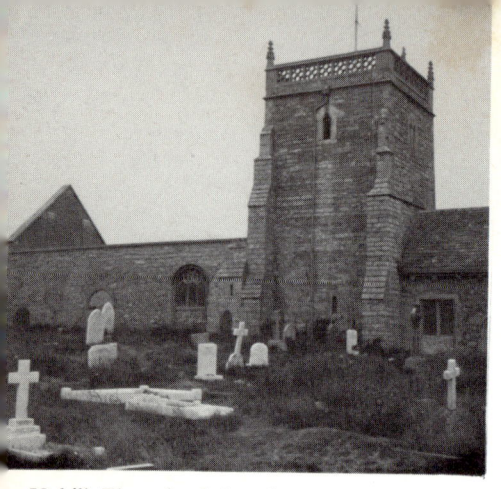

Uphill. The ruined church.

Lympsham. The entrance to the Manor House—interesting Tudor pastiche.

Lympsham. The Wharf.

East Brent. The War Memorial.

Bleadon. Fishermen on the Axe.

Bleadon. The Old Well House.

stormbeached timber of every shape and size. Thrifty locals often artfully utilise these offerings, constructing garden gates, ramshackle sheds, or benches for the convenience of plaster gnomes.

From time to time—though infrequently nowadays—the remains of drowned sailors are uncovered. A dune is shifted and the bones it has embalmed for years are left brittle and moistureless. In the eighteenth century, it was the custom to bury such mortal driftwood at a point just above the high tide mark, but by 1800 a new act was passed entitling more respectful treatment—'Where dead bodies are cast on shore from the seas, the churchwardens or overseers of the Parish, or in extra parochial places, the constable or head-borough, are to remove the bodies to some convenient place, and there cause them to be buried in the churchyard.' As at other funerals, the minister, parish clerk, and sexton, performed their respective duties, the cost being incurred by the parish concerned.

The waves here have an individual appeal. Although they lack the vitreous lustre of those on the southern coast, they too are transformed by sunlight, and, in dull weather even, can make a fine sight, hissing and splitting, flattening and advancing in crumpled sheets of frost and silver grey.

The level tidal stretch of sand is utilised by drivers who regard it as a sort of poor man's Brand's Hatch. Speed limit signs are erected at regular intervals, and on a cold November's day it is not unusual to be confronted with people re-enacting Fangio fantasies in mini cars or sober family saloons.

During the summer months the Brean Leisure Centre offers a variety of activities ranging from the prosaic (International Wrestling) to the bizarre (Roman Chariot Racing). A further attraction is the Daily Dolphin Show providing a unique opportunity for these intelligent creatures to observe human beings strolling around completely unfettered, eating, drinking, calling out to each other, and—if the weather's conducive—indulging in preliminary courtship rituals.

* * *

Extending seaward is a wide and level expanse of mud called the Berrow Flats. In sunny weather they are scarred by glittering streaks of water where the tide has retreated and provide an excellent feeding ground for scavenging gulls, curlew and redshank, oystercatchers and dunlin.

To the south the sandy areas broaden and transverse dunes rise to a height of over fifty feet. Basically they are formed by the piling-up of blown sand against obstacles, and it is necessary, if they are to be both preserved and controlled, to arrest their movement. About 1890 sea buckthorn was planted in this area, and this has resulted in a rash of new vegetation. Formerly this district consisted of extensive tracts of grey-green marram grass, but now alder, sallow, willow and brambles have secured a foothold. Spartina grass also, spreading from the north, is 'fixing' the mud-flats and encouraging the growth of fresh dunes.

This hardy perennial plant, technically known as *Spartina Townsendii*, was first planted in Bridgwater Bay in 1929. The grass grows on mud and reclaims land from the sea by retaining tidal silt. But now, like the prickly pear in Australia, it has got out of control and is spreading across the sandy areas. In 1964, in an attempt to curb its rapid advance, Sand Bay was sprayed with chemicals from a helicopter, but this, apart from being only partially successful, proved expensive and harmful to wild life. The problem remains.

Another effective soil-gripper is the Mat-grass. Before the other vegetation had established itself, this was the principal deterrent to wind erosion around these shores. In the reign of George II, an Act of Parliament was passed forbidding the cutting or removal of this plant. A fine of twenty-five shillings was imposed upon anyone who flouted this law. In default of payment, the punishment became increasingly harsh: three months imprisonment with hard labour. This measure similarly applied to anyone caught in possession of the grass within a five mile radius of any spot where it happened to be growing. Why on earth, one might reasonably enquire, would one want to bother to steal the wretched weed in the first place? Well, although the grass has no nutritional value, its tough fibrous texture could be adapted for numerous practical purposes. These are often listed in the older botanical works. Withering's compendium is a point in instance:

> Triandria—Digynia—Arunds arenaria—Sea Reed, Mat Grass—Sea—Bent; Calyx one flowered, a little longer than the corolla; panicle close, leaves involute, pungent. Root creeping, often twenty feet long; straw stiff, greenish yellow; leaves very long, mostly radical; panicle close, linear, attenuated at each end; chaff-scales unequal, membraneous, rough on the keel, very few of the seeds are perfected. This plant is common on the coast where ever there is loose sand, which it serves to bind down by its long tough roots. It is manufactured into door mats and floor brushes. In the Hebrides it is made into ropes for various uses; mats for pack saddles, bags and vessels for holding and preparing meal and grain, and into hats; it has also been planted in the Outer Hebrides for curing sand drift—Perennial; flowers in July; Eng. Boty., Vol. VIII, pl. 520.

As for the Sea Buckthorn, that too is a plant with character: savage, grasping and prickly, it is most painful to wade through on foot, and, if in league with the bramble, tends to etch spontaneous compositions across one's legs. Despite such an aggressive disposition, it puts on a good show in winter. Then its dusty copper leaves, starred by galaxies of orange berries, scald the pale sand-hills with a coverlet of living fire.

Inland from the dune country, rich alluvial grasslands extend from the Mendips to the Quantocks, and trees and hedgerows become more commonplace. By the roadside, in waste places, and on neglected land, the Ragwort is plentiful. The country folk here, on account of their vivid golden flowerheads, call them 'yallers'; up in Scotland, they are more abusively termed as 'Stinking Willies'. This is a reference to the plant's rank odour when crushed or bruised.

* * *

Some people, on hearing the terms 'dunes' and 'slacks', are uncertain as to what precisely these distinctions imply. The classifications are slightly academic. On the beach, rising above the tideswept areas, are the dunes, usually stabilised by Marram Grass, Sea Spurge, Couch Grass and other flora. Often they are referred to as 'mobile' dunes. This is because the south westerlies, dislodging the surface layer of sand, carry it inland to re-shape itself over again; and so, by degrees, a whole succession of dunes slowly accumulate, following up behind one another like waves on a beach. This process is checked by the planting of suitable vegetation; even so, the measure is by no means always successful. A 'blow-out' sometimes occurs where the vegetation has been unable to retain the sand, and the wind, digging and uprooting, has stripped the flora to its base leaving only the exposed tentacles of plants.

Backing the dune area are the 'slacks', tiny trough-like depressions where small quantities of water have collected attracting an individual flora of their own: Skull Cap, Dog Violet, Silverweed, and a whole variety of butterflies are seen here in summer. Where these hollows are slightly more pronounced, the moisture has collected sufficiently to form pools. These are often enclosed by true Bullrushes, and plants such as the Marsh Pennywort, the Meadowsweet and various species of orchid.

* * *

Between Brean and Berrow, exposed at low tide, there is an oval space of sand enclosed by blackened timbers. Puncturing the beach like the jaws of some gat-toothed old shark, these rotted old ribs comprise the mortal remains of the *Nornen*, a 1,000-ton Norwegian barque, which, after breaking her anchors off Lundy Island, was driven ashore amid rough tides and swivelling snow on March 3rd, 1897. When the came aground on the Berrow Flats, her captain, aided by ropes thrown to him by local people, managed to struggle to the mainland. His crew, however, wary of the crashing waves, waited some hours until the John Godfery Morris—the Burnham lifeboat active at that period—transferred them and the ship's dog to the foreshore. As for the *Nornen*, it was found that the barque could not be refloated; all her sails had been torn down and her timbers were damaged. Eventually it was decided to dismantle her on the site, and this was subsequently done, leaving only the pathetic underbelly of the craft protruding above the sands to this day. One significant souvenir of this vessel, the figurehead, was retained in the area, and may be seen adorning the entrance to a Berrow cottage which has been named accordingly.

The Berrow Flats, as has been noted, attracts a large number of wading birds which feed there in winter. Bridgwater Bay, more curiously, is renowned as a moulting-ground for huge flocks of Shelducks. Why, season after season, do these strikingly beautiful birds accumulate at this single spot? The question has been teasing naturalists for centuries. Some think it is a question of instinct proving more powerful than environmental change. One explanation goes that, during the Ice Age, the vast glacial sheet terminated somewhere north of this area, and the flocks of Shelducks, having never varied their migratory pattern, still continue to flock to this area, avoiding the long-melted blanket of cold.

Venturing on the actual flats themselves are fishermen digging for lugworm. One cannot help paying a tribute to the remarkable *objets d'art* created by these delightful wrigglers: miniature sandy pinnacles, tiny reefs, trees branching numerous tubular stems, all cemented together and held intact by the secretions of their bodies—they are the true Buckminster Fullers of our age.

Sometimes, after a strong tide, outcrops of bluish-grey clay are left exposed on the mudflats. This silt was first deposited in the huge valley occupying the ground between the Quantocks and the Mendips in 6000 B.C. and helped to raise the land to near its present height. When these ancient mudflats dried out, they were invaded by plant life. Open pools were colonised, first by aquatic plants, and, at the edges, by clumps of rushes. The latter, fencing in the central watery areas, rapidly spread outwards. Decaying remains of plant and insect life gradually accumulated on the beds of these pools, absorbing moisture, filling-in the depressions and drying-out the ground. In fact, many authorities agree that, had not Sedgemoor's marshes been constantly replenished by tidal floods and high precipitation, the land would have followed the normal course, reverting to grassland and carr vegetation. However, around 3000 B.C, a change in the climate occurred. The rainfall increased, and, by washing calcium compounds and other precious salts from the soil, effected a chemical change in the nature of the marsh: soil became poorer, wetter and thinner; the eutrophic transition to grass and woodland was halted; organic material built up steadily in the centre of these swamps; the water-table rose, and the vast boggy areas widened outwards, leaving areas such as the Mendips, Quantocks and Poldens, the isolated knolls at Brent and Glastonbury, islanded among a dense fretwork of reeds and sedges.

Later, these waters were to support a vast number of living organisms, and, in the twelfth century, Glastonbury Abbey owned rich fisheries on Sedgemoor, such as the one at Clewer, which harvested some 7,000 eels, and other profitable holdings at Nyland and Middlezoy. Only after centuries of embankment building, together with the enlistment of Dutch engineers, did Somerset's fens come to resemble good farming land.

* * *

The village of Berrow, now practically merged with Burnham, is built upon loam with a clay subsoil. Lost among the undulating sand hummocks, the parish church of Saint Mary has a Jacobean gallery dated 1637 and an embattled western tower containing a peal of bells. The present edifice was clearly built upon an earlier one, for, in the churchyard, are the ancient figures of a knight and his lady and the base of a fourteenth-century cross.

Mainly modern, those eager for the distant past are not likely to be detained by the houses of Berrow for any great length. Anyone absolutely hell-bent on finding something of antiquarian interest, however, might like to visit Barton Farm and sample the olfactory delights of the 100-year-old Welsh-type pig sty, designated for preservation as an agricultural monument of lasting integrity. Other buildings include Ellen's Cottages, a charity row erected in 1868. The Court House, between the Berrow Road and the dunes, where two skeletons were dug up many years ago, was demolished.

If one discounts tangible relics, however, and wishes to trace the history of the actual parish, it is possible to go back a long way. In ancient documents, Berrow appears variously as 'Berges', 'Berve' and 'Berrough', and, like its neighbour Brean, it was one of the manors granted by the Conqueror to the Norman knight, Walter de Dowai, for services rendered in the subjugation of these islands. Collinson, in his account, sketches in a few terse details of its history up until 1791—'King William Rufus granted the manor, with that of Burrington, to the abbey of Glastonbury, which grant was confirmed by King Henry I, and afterwards by Pope Alexander, in 1168. After the dissolution, it was granted to Edward, Duke of Somerset, and in the schedule of the whole estate it is set down at the yearly value of £45 1s. It now belongs to Sir John Stanley Bart, whose father, Sir Edward Stanley, purchased it off William Whitchurch, esq., of Nunney.'

BURNHAM

VIEWING Burnham from the northern vantage point, one sees the old lighthouse, red-striped and upright on matchstick legs, and behind it, a succession of pale facades overlooking oat-coloured sand and gradually receding into a blurr of shadow-shapes. No outstanding feature strikes the eye. There is a pavilion with a large white curvy roof, protruding like a gigantic topping of whipped cream, otherwise nothing but the corroded remnants of a marine lake, the squat mouse-coloured church tower, and the line of neutral boarding-houses dissolving into nothing.

In the 1830s, following the lead of other towns, an attempt was made to establish this desolate outpost as a spa after the local rector, the Reverend David Davies, discovered mineral springs there. Regrettably one outflow proved revolting on the palate and somewhat less than crystal clear. A chemical analysis summed up its properties with admirable succintness—'The water was turbid and slightly yellow. The smell was very offensive, resembling that of a cess-pool, mixed with an odour not unlike horseradish.'

If Burnham never prospered as a spa, it has trudged along contentedly as a seaside resort. It is—according to one writer—the perfect ideal of the average Sunday School Manager, seeking a suitable place for the school's annual treat. Undeniably, it is a tolerable enough spot in its way, and its celebrated straddle-legged lighthouse seems to have won a place of affection in many writer's hearts. Set at the eastern end of Bridgwater Bay, which Ptolemy called the Estuary of the Uzella, it is eleven miles from Weston-super-Mare and twenty-eight from Bristol. The climate is astringent and bracing; sand is plentiful and bathing safe; facilities for hiring power and rowing boats are available, and there is an excellent golf course. On the seafront are diversions including mechanical toys for children, roundabouts,

Burnham   The Old Lighthouse around 1800

Burnham   The Old Lighthouse

trampolines, an amusement arcade and a crazy golf course. From the shore, it is possible to discern the gas-cooled reactor and cooling towers of Hinkley Point station floating in the misty distance, like an updated vision of Camelot.

The name of the town is usually attributed thus: 'burne' signifying home, 'ham' denoting a curve in a river. But this is hardly an adequate description of Burnham's situation, for the resort—far from huddling on a river bend, defiantly abuts against the Channel. Unlike Portishead or Clevedon, it nestles in no cove or bay, but is a stark wall of houses, overlooking at low tide the senile dribblings of the Parrett.

Burnham also has a pier, 900 feet long, formerly linked with the railway terminus. George Reed, the so-called 'father of Burnham-on-Sea,' laid the foundation stone in 1857 and it was officially opened in the following year. The accumulation of tidal silt renders it now unsuitable for pleasure steamers, but formerly a regular Cardiff service operated. One of the earliest of these vessels, the iron paddler, *The Ruby*, was built in 1854 at Renfrew, and, after putting in three years service with the Burnham Harbour Company, was sold in 1864. By some curious quirk of fate, she ended up as a blockade runner in the American Civil War. The last of the boats, *The Sherbro*, after years of illustrious duty harassing West Africa's slave trade, was acquired by Burnham in 1884 and plied back and forth until 1888 when she was sold.

The rail system that backed up the pier, the blue-engined 'Somerset and Dorset Line', had an individual reputation. To its devotees and regular passengers, it was dubbed the 'Slow and Dirty', in that it displayed these two qualities in abundance. A juror, who had been fined by a judge for non-attendance, was granted remittance at Wells Assize after he attributed his lateness to the rail service. On hearing that the unfortunate man had travelled by this rough and ready line, his Lordship considered he had already suffered punishment enough.

* * *

Apart from some cottages of late Georgian to early Victorian origin, the town is not overburdened with items of antiquarian or architectural interest. The parish church of Saint Andrew, standing near the seashore and dating from 1316, contains component parts of an altar-piece designed by Inigo Jones.

Burnham, originally, was a royal manor. King Alfred was the owner, and, stemming from this fact, it would seem probable that there was a church standing here in the ninth century A.D. When Alfred died, he left a will bequeathing the manor to be shared between his son and nephew.

A Herefordshire dignitary, Harold of Ewias, owned the advowson of the church in 1100 A.D. He made a generous gift to the abbey of St. Peter's of Gloucestershire, which, among other contributions, included the whole of the tithe of Burnham and Brean—'And of Burnham, in particular, the whole tithe of hay and of meadow-pence and of eels, little and big.'

The connection with St Peter's was sustained for over two centuries, and then, by license of Edward I, the advowson was granted to Bishop Robert Burnell of Wells. This gift, along with a yearly pension of £10 which St Peter's used to receive from Burnham, was confirmed by the King, on the eve of his Scottish campaign at Berwick-on-Tweed in 1290.

Burnell was a leading man of his time: statesman, ecclesiastic and close personal friend of the King, it was, in the opinion of S. G. Nash,* his influence brought to bear on the monarch which resulted in the advowson of St Andrew's being returned to its rightful diocese.

One of the church's most distinctive features are its sculptures. They were formerly part of an elaborate baroque altarpiece commissioned by James II for the chapel of Whitehall Palace. Designed by Inigo Jones, they were carved by Grinling Gibbons and his assistant, Quellin, and comprised a tableau of fat cherubs encircling the proclamation—'Glory to God in the Highest and on Earth Peace, Good Will towards Men.' Flanking this arrangement were two angels, mounted on pedestals, their pinions taut and ready to flap, their eyes cast shamefacedly downwards. Subsequently this altarpiece was moved to Westminster Abbey and placed behind the High Altar. It remained there until 1820, when, because of its incongruity or Catholic overtones, the Dean and Chapter had it moved yet again. About this time, the Bishop of Rochester, who was also the Vicar of Burnham, acquired it and used fragments to decorate the Chancel of St Andrew's. Nowadays it is dispersed over various parts of the interior of the building, the Nave windows, behind the Altar and in the Baptistry.

* * *

North of the church are two of the town's most distinctive landmarks. The High Lighthouse, on the Berrow Road, was erected to warn seamen of the Gore Sands; it is 120 feet tall and gives flashes of two and a half seconds. A smaller lighthouse-on-stilts occupies a prominent position on the sands and has an endearingly eccentric appearance.

The history of these lights is interesting, but not luminously clear. The first official lighthouse was built in 1800 at the request and subscription of the Rev. D. Davies, the curate to Dr Walter King, the Bishop of Rochester. It was a plain round tower standing on the esplanade, 'the original pharos, the great feature of the place, and the cynosure of the waters'—as Dr Henning wittily described it.

A story attributes its origin to the concern of a local fisherman's wife over her husband's safety. Every night she would hang a lamp by the window of her cottage, so that local craft might receive some indication of their whereabouts. When the old couple died, local mariners and fisherfolk, lamenting the loss of this modest sparkler, decided that it should be replaced by a permanent structure.

This is a pleasing legend with possibly an iota of truth in it, but the major factor culminating in the construction of Burnham's light was undoubtedly the fairly frequent spectacle of human carcasses strewn along the beach. And it is this theme which is re-echoed by Frances Wood, in her reminiscences of

---

* 'The Story of Burnham Church'—by S. G. Nash.

the village during the middle years of the nineteenth century. Quicksands, she writes, were a hazard on Burnham beach, and there was a particularly treacherous stretch lying between the wooden lighthouse and the shore. She recalls how a 'dapper' friend of hers got stuck in them, and—had it not been for her crinolines keeping her afloat—nearly lost her life. A man, eventually, hauled her out. 'Underneath she was as black as Burnham mud could make her, but outside she looked as if turned out of a bandbox, a regular whited sepulchre.'

After meditating on the growing commercialism of Burnham, and the shifting mud and sand of its shoreline, she relates a curious story, the gist of which runs as follows. She and her brother and sister were digging sandcastles on the beach. An old clergyman was picking his way across the sand, and, unwittingly, he stopped within inches of a large trench they had recently excavated. When they pulled him aside and warned him of the danger, he explained that he was blind and sat down and genially chatted with the children. Had they ever heard, he enquired, the story of Burnham's lighthouses, and so, like a less fanatical Ancient Mariner, he reeled off a tidy little yarn.

Many years ago, he said, there was an old man, who was Rector of Burnham and lived at the Colony, a substantial residence overlooking the sea. His life, however, was made a misery by the sight of so many drowned men washed up by his house. Nightly he would pray for the ships negotiating this stretch of coast, imploring God to grant them a safe passage round the Wolf Sands, but, eventually, deciding to put action before spiritual entreaties, he purchased the most powerful lamp obtainable and set it up by his window. Contacting the Port of Bristol Authority, he asked them to inform all sailors concerned of his course of action, so that, on seeing his warning signal, they would interpret it correctly. The ploy, it seems, proved effective, and for the next few years the drownings and shipwrecks sharply declined. But still, nightly, the old cleric maintained his vigil, lighting the lamp, praying, denying himself rest, until, one morning, he was found on his knees dead, the lamp extinguished beside him.

The young rector who succeeded him, the story continued, was indifferent to coastguard duties and neglected to maintain the light. So the situation relapsed, deaths mounted again, and, eventually, Trinity House intervened and erected the pillar lighthouse. Yet, afterwards, they discovered that they had selected too low a vantage point to take into account the massive rise and fall of the tides, and so, to complement it, they built the lighthouse-on-legs. The two illuminants, the powerful new beam working in conjunction with the pilot light of the smaller fabric, served their purpose admirably.

This account is, of course, peppered with inaccuracies and ignores the seminal role of David Davies in this affair, but, conversely, it does pay tribute to the fact that earlier clerics had a hand in Burnham's safety-at-sea campaign. Margery Sanders, in her diverting study of the village, writes that a sexton of the seventeen-fifties, after tipping the fisherman's wife £5, proceeded to erect a light on the church tower. When the Reverend Davies appeared on the scene, he—Mrs Sanders states—gave the sexton a further £20 and started to re-organise matters along his own lines. It is a well-attested fact that it was he, not Trinity House, who first took the lighthouse matter in hand and had the original crude beacon put up. This act also empowered him to levy dues upon all vessels passing the light, and in this manner he acquired a sum of money which came in very useful during his later, less successful, spa and bath-house experiments.

Nonetheless, in 1829 the Corporation of Trinity House decided that Burnham should be fitted with an up-to-date lighthouse, so, after paying David Davies £13,500 by way of compensation, they commenced the building of the pillar and wooden lighthouses respectively. The former fabric was over a hundred feet high, paraffin-fire, with four silvered copper reflectors and adjustable shutters. It became, in a modest way, a tourist attraction and many visitors toiled up the spiral staircase to gain a view of Newport and the Foreland north of Ilfracombe.

Yet there were, inevitably, still many losses, nearly all of which were attributable to the Gore Sands: Captain Burnell, his crew of three, and his grandson, aged eight, sank with his ship, *Mary*, and its cargo of coal, the *John*, the *Edward* and *Margaret*—all were overwhelmed by this swirling all-engulfing layer of water and sand.

Regarded coolly, however, Burnham, without jagged rocks or tricky tide-races, was not a section of coast which should have presented especial difficulties to the skilled navigator. The main danger lay in a vessel, owing to strong winds or misjudgement, getting caught up in the mud and sand of the shallows and heeling over and getting smothered by the tide. And when this occurred, lives were liberally lost, or—if luck intervened—a rescue might take place.

On the seawall is a tablet, written in a convoluted style, recording the bravery of five men:

IN COMMEMORATION OF THE HUMANE AND INTREPID CONDUCT OF CHARLES HUNT, MASTER OF THE *FAME* OF THIS PORT, FREDERICK REES AND DAVID DAVIES, HIS CREW WHO ON 1st MARCH, 1836, AFTER MAKING A MOST HAZARDOUS BUT UNSUCCESSFUL ATTEMPT TO SAVE THE LIVES OF THE CREW OF THE *MARGARET* AND BEING AFTERWARDS JOINED BY JAMES SHARMAN AND FREDERICK COOMBS, VOLUNTEERS OF EQUAL MERIT UNAPPALLED BY INTENSE DARKNESS, A TREMENDOUS GALE AND A RAGING SEA, EMBARKED FROM THIS BEACH IN A SMALL BOAT TO THE RESCUE OF THE MASTER AND GREATER PART OF THE CREW OF THE *MOSS ROSE* OF BRIDGWATER WHICH LAY WRECKED ON THE GORE SAND, WHERE THEY MUST HAVE UNDOUBTEDLY PERISHED HAD NOT THE PERILOUS AND LAUDABLE ENDEAVOURS OF THE ABOVE NAMED PERSONS THROUGH DARING ASSISTANCE HAPPILY PREVENTED IT. THIS TABLET IS ERECTED BY SUBSCRIPTION AS A TESTIMONY OF PUBLIC APPLAUSE AND AS A STIMULUS TO OTHERS ON LIKE UNFORTUNATE OCCASIONS TO FOLLOW THE EXAMPLE OF THOSE BRAVE DELIVERERS AND TO DO LIKEWISE.

Bridgwater, after this rescue, awarded Burnham with its first lifeboat, thus inaugurating a necessary and long-lasting institution. The boat was first stored by the wooden lighthouse. Subsequently it was moved to a resting-place near the station. It reclined on a launching cradle which ran on rails down to the pierhead.

In 1866, Cheltenham, that sedate and prosperous spa, kindly footed the bill for Burnham's first Royal National Lifeboat, which, quite rightly, bore her name. She was thirty-five feet long, a standard self-righter, with ten oars and carrying a crew of twelve. The launching took place on October 22nd of the same year.

Her first service was in aid of the *Prudence*, a Watchet craft, which, after attempting to enter the Parrett estuary while the tide was on the ebb, got caught up in a strong wind and was driven aground on Steart Island. So violent was the pummelling and pounding this schooner received, that, despite the shallow water, she was jerked and shifted a distance of three miles. When the *Cheltenham* reached her, the crew, drenched and desperate, were clinging to the bowsprit while the tide roared across the decking.

* * *

Strictly speaking, Burnham has few architectural highlights proper. The town is approached from the east through rows of neat cubicle-like semis in the functional-brutalist style. Red brick is a popular building material around these parts and variegates the aspect of many Tudor suburban residence. The houses on the seafront, the observant visitor will note, are slightly showier and more opulent, but even they somehow lack the finish and assurance of their counterparts at Weston, to whom they have the air of being down-at-heel relatives.

In fact, Burnham's esplanade presents a somewhat irregular skyline. Regarded from the southern end of the beach, the quoins and Tuscan columns of the Queen's Hotel gradually melt into Jacobean gables and a rather drab block called Kinver Terrace. These give way to the parish church and the Daviesville Terrace, low, boxy, white-fronted and structurally inharmonious. The northern tip is redeemed by Catherine Terrace, tall, handsome, honey-coloured, with triangular pediments and a pierced balustrade—the finest secular edifice in the town.

An approximate chronology of some of these buildings might run along the following lines. The Clarence Hotel, in the centre of the esplanade—a seemly black and white structure—appears to have been the first guest-paying establishment to have been erected. Shortly afterwards, around 1830 or thereabouts, the Bath-House complex materialised from the remnants of the original lighthouse. Other blocks of houses were to follow, Kinver Terrace, in 1843; also, at that period, Regent Street and the Baptist Chapel.

Then, in 1846, the Custom House, not far from the pier, was erected. Ships docking locally would report to the officers of Her Majesty's Customs stationed here, and dues would be payed and transferred to Bridgwater. The latter borough, in the minds of patriotic Burnham citizens, was rapidly acquiring the status of an ogre. She had the monopoly of all the coastal trade, and, to little Burnham's evident disgust, resented the idea of sharing it with the smaller communities. A rather tart comment in the 1859 tourist handbook refers to this matter:

> The town is not only rendering no accommodation whatever, for the convenience of vessels at Burnham, but having actually spent a large sum in parliamentary opposition to its projected improvements.

The decade heralded by 1850 was perhaps significant as the years of George Reed, the town's foremost citizen, developer, philanthropist and industrialist. The National School, a charitable foundation, was financed by him and bears a marble tablet describing its function:

> The National School Establishment was erected in the year of our Lord 1855, by George Reed, Esquire, of this Town, and given in Trust for the Benefit and Education of the children of the Poor Inhabitants of this Parish.

At the south end of the esplanade, he erected two quadrant terraces, one a beautiful Classically-styled row, the other, a more severe and restrained block, and named them after his two daughters, Catherine and Julia respectively. Reed's efforts were by no means contained here. He also financed the construction of the Reed's Arms, now the Queen's Hotel, a fussy Italianate concoction, the original name of which may still be discerned in the stonework.

Reed was influential, too, as a director of the Somerset and Dorset Railway and gave it financial backing during difficult periods. He loaned the line money on no interest terms, and, in 1865, actually sold them one of his locomotives for £1,450. Predictably he was a moving light in the subsidiary concern, the 'Burnham Tidal Harbour and Railway Company', the objectives of which were to expand Burnham's facilities as a port and railhead. Yet, it must be admitted that the aims of this company were a trifle optimistic, and, although there was a small amount of trade between here and South Wales, mainly dealing in coal and agricultural produce, the very considerable accumulation and movement of tidal silt rendered Burnham hopelessly impractical for any large-scale marine operations. Highbridge, however, for a period, fared slightly better, and local bricks and tiles, turf, manure and dairy products were traded regularly against Welsh iron and coal.

* * *

One or two of the buildings in Burnham, because of their architectural or historic interest, deserve to be considered in some detail. One of these, Stert House, is a sturdy Regency fabric on the promenade, with green shutters and moulting whitewash. This was formerly the Bath-House, the principal component in 'Daviesville', the spa that never was.

Flushed with the success of his lighthouse venture, the Reverend David Davies started to follow up his conviction that Burnham possessed mineral springs. He had already noted similarities in the soil with that of Cheltenham and hoped to find further resemblances in the fluids sealed between the underlying rock-stratas.

He hired drilling equipment and work was begun. When the men dug beneath the sand to a depth of eight feet, they uncovered a deposit of black greasy loam. On removing this, a thin sheet of quicksand running in veins was exposed. This rested on a layer of hard clay, twenty-five feet thick, which softened on contact with the upper air. Finally, they reached an equally bulky layer of blue clay, which, when mixed with vinegar, effervesced and produced carbonic gas. In the meantime, at the bottom of the shaft, cloudy-yellow water had begun to seep through and fill the intervening space. This, too, was analysed, and it transpired that two springs had been discovered, within yards of each other, one saline chalybeate, the other sulphurous.

After a satisfactory machinery for drawing the mineral waters up had been devised, the Reverend Davies, hoping to create another Harrogate or Tunbridge, erected a complex of buildings around the wells, but fashion, capricious lass that she is, refused to be compromised by such chemotherapeutic overtures. Even the fact that Doctor Henning had written a thesis about these springs did not sustain trade. And yet, to give the spa its due, it did enjoy a brief celebrity, and, for a few years, coaches rattled in from the Midlands and South Wales discharging cargoes of convalescents. They, no doubt, would be graciously welcomed by the Reverend Davies or the physician in charge. The last of these bath superintendents, Doctor Beverley Morris, received a steady supply of mail praising their curative powers. One elderly judge, in particular, set great store by Burnham spa-water. Even while holidaying on the continent, he would carry with him bottles containing this stimulating substance; in fact—he confided to Doctor Morris—he was loath to undertake any long journey without them. He was convinced that, in his plain glass containers, the genii of health was securely corked.

Another local residence, Saint Anne's, is notable as the former home of the lawyer and politician, George Cave. He had a varied political career, serving as a Unionist M.P. for Kingston, then, in 1915, he was promoted to Solicitor General. A year later he was appointed Home Secretary. Finally, he terminated his career as Lord Chancellor, a post which he filled almost up to his death on March 29th, 1929. The Caves were evidently a popular couple at Burnham, and many of the residents seem to have retained fond memories of them. The Reverend E. H. Smith, writing in 1945, waxes quite lyrical over the idyllic quality of their relationship. Whenever he mentions their house, he is affected by a heady onslaught of sentimental recollections:

> At the northern end of the ladies' golf links is a notable house, with white frontage and lovely gardens running right down to the sea, where some years ago the Lord Chancellor of England, Lord Cave, and his wife, Lady Estella Cave, lived in love and close companionship. They loved Burnham and worshipped regularly in the little church at Berrow.

Not far away is the Colony. With its thatching and Tudor gables, this was formerly a very attractive building, but a fire in the eighteen-nineties necessitated the installation of a tiled roof and other minor modifications. A delicate pink-toned sketch of it made around 1859, however, depicts it in its architectural prime. Certain of its features recall the old English cottage and farmhouse styles to be later popularised by architects such as Voysey. The layout comprises a total of four interlinked buildings. It is said to have been modelled upon the ships of the period, the projecting poops and forecastles of which correspond roughly to the taller east and west wings of the complex. Built in the latter half of the eighteenth century, its original owner is said to have been a retired sea captain. He had four daughters, the story goes, who were forever quarrelling, and so he devised a building which, while bearing in mind their filial bonds, ensured that each of them could enjoy the maximum of privacy.

* * *

Burnham's history, apart from the floods, is happily uncluttered by cataclysms and violent upheavals. The Domesday Record of the parish is a characteristically droll assemblage of details relating to acreage, manpower and meadowland comprising the holding:

Walter himself holds Burnham. Brixi held it in the time of King Edward, and gelded for four hides. The arable is twelve carucates: one carucate is in demesne, and three servants, and seven villeins, and eight cottagers with five ploughs. There are one hundred and fifty acres of meadow, and twenty acres of pasture. It is worth four pounds.

Walter was, of course, the over-endowed Walter de Dowai, the Norman knight, who, after the Conquest, acquired the parish along with Bridgwater, Brean and Berrow. From this point, historical matters runs a little thin, but, to take up the story many years later, in the reign of Henry III, we learn that the tenure had been acquired by Robert de Mucegros in 'free socage'* of the heirs of Henry Fitz-Richard. Mention of it again occurs during the thirteenth year of Edward I's reign, when, the present lord of the manor, John Tregoz, procured a charter of 'free warren' in his demesne.

In the fourteenth century, the moiety of Burnham and Burnham Moor belonged to William Lord Grandison. On his death, it passed to Peter, his eldest son, who died in 1357. He left no son or daughter, and his brother, John Grandison, Bishop of Exeter, inherited the estate. When he died in 1369, his nephew, William Montague, Earl of Salisbury, was found to be the next heir. Other owners followed in succession, the Allots, Ropers and Pophams, until, in the eighteenth century, it was purchased by Sir Copplestone Warwick Bamfylde Bart. It was his son, Richard, who, in 1760, began to sell off the estate to its various leaseholders. This practice was continued by Sir Charles Bampfylde Bart, who held the tenure at the time of Collinson's survey. He sold off the remaining 400 acres to three Burnham farmers in 1792 for around £1,500.

One significant occurrence interrupted this narrative—the disastrous

---

* Meaning the tenants—'sokemen'—had distinct obligations of service.

flood of January 1607. An immense tidal wave roared over the sea-wall, and this great foaming fleece spread across the entire levels of Huntspill, Berrow, South and East Brent. It captured the imagination of the nation and was the subject of a London pamphlet—'God's Warning to His People of England'—interpreting it as a divine omen. Extraordinary sights were witnessed. Rats and mice, desperate to escape baptism, scrambled onto the backs of sheep, cows, swine and even milkmaids; and clusters of people and animals herded together on high ground, as the huge rippling sheet swirled and hissed around them. Like parties recently disembarked from the Ark, they stood rapt, shoulder to shoulder with beasts they sheared and slaughtered, and watched the sea reclaim its lost possessions.

At the time of the 1891 inspection, the village presented a sombre sight. A few cottages huddled around the church, which, on the south and west side, was bounded by the massive sea-wall. At low tide, the yellow sands of the estuary lay stripped and cold; fishermen, employing butts and hangs, trapped thousands of salmon there. The planting of sedge and buckthorn had begun to establish stability on the sand-hills, but, during gales, there was still enough loose material blown about to half bury some of the low seaward-facing dwellings. Clearly the antiquarian found its situation, as ever, bleak, raw and remote. In fact, his description of Burnham beach is a fine piece of evocative prose, much of which still holds good today, although the rabbit population has possibly depleted:

> The situation of that part of the village of Burnham which is near the church is very bleak and cold, being exposed to the north-westerly winds, which, blowing over the channel, are very unfriendly to vegetation. The coast is a fine sandy beach, which, when the tide is at the ebb, is half a mile in breadth. The upper part of it next the land rises in high sand-banks, ridge behind ridge, forming a strong natural fortification or entrenchment, which the highest tide never passes nor breaks through. Multitudes of rabbits make these banks their residence, and the ground in many places is almost covered with the shells of the small land helix and viparious snail. Most of the plants which are generally found on our coast adorn the beach, particularly the yellow poppy, shrubby stone crop, and diverse other kinds, with a variety of lichen and other mosses.

But what of the people? We find nothing in Collinson relating to the hamlet's occupants; his accounts are brisk and surgical. For information as to what type of people lived in the parish, what they did, how they spent their time and money, it is necessary to consult Richard Locke, historian, inspired agriculturalist and founder of the Burnham Society. His writings on the community are enlivened by a wealth of social detail to be found nowhere else. Life stirs in the paper bones of his recollections:

> Burnham within memory of its old inhabitants was an inconsiderable parish of poor renters and cottagers who existed without hot dinners, silk clothing, carriages of pleasure, mahogany furniture, clocks watches or even Tea kettles, notwithstanding the profusion of these at present. The

Lympsham. Church Farm.

...npsham. The Manor House. One of ornamental pinnacles.

Lympsham. The Manor House. A remnant of a Hermit's Chapel or some nondescript folly?

Berrow Parish C[hurch] embattled and ru[gged] dominates the wi[nd] ravaged expanse [of] the dunes.

The badly-eroded carved monuments to a knight and his lady —almost certainly contemporary with the 14th Century church that stood here.

Berrow. The figure[head] head of the Norner[?] decorates one of t[he] cottages.

Burnham.
Steart House.

...nham. A carnival
...t is in progress
... power boat race.
... faint pencil line of
... Island can just
... made out.

Burnham. St.
Andrew's Church.
The tower is late
14th Century; the
pulpit is Jacobean;
the North Aisle and
the Gallery were
added in 1838.

Burnham. Huge concrete blocks embedded in the sands to counter wave-erosion.

Burnham. The High Lighthouse.

Burnham. The Low Lighthouse. "A continuous light is given from the low wooden structure on the sands, familiarly known as the lighthouse on legs. Mariners have to steer into such a position that both lights are brought into line before their vessels enter the river, if they wish to avoid imitating the example of Alfred the Great who is alleged to have been wrecked upon Gore Sands." (Bristol Mercury 'Cheap Guide to Burnham-on-Sea' 1884).

ham. Clarence Hotel.

Burnham. A section of the 'Colony'. Now a rather ungainly slather of rooftops and gables, early sketches reveal it as a charming essay in Victorian Tudor.

Burnham. Catherine Terrace.

Burnham. Julia Terrace.

Tom Coryate's Tomb, north of Surat, India.

Wells. Beechbarrow. Gaetano Celestra, an Italian P.O.W., erected this powerful representation of Romulus and Remus being suckled by the She-wolf to honour his wife who was killed in an air raid.

Barwick. The Spire: one of England's purest follies.

Burrow Mump—from an old sketch.

The Cross, Shepton Mallet

pton Mallet. The Market Cross.

Andrew Crosse, electrician, poet—the notorious "Thunder-and-Lightning Man" of Broomfield—huddles over his lately-devised acari.

The original arrangement of the Marble Altar Piece of Grinling Gibbons and Quellin in the Sanctuary, with acknowledgements to the Somerset Archaeological and Natural History Society.

farmers carried their dinners to market in their pockets in the same way as labourers carry them to the field at present, and the coats they wore as well as their family blankets were the produce of their flocks spun by their wives and daughters.

Locke, taking pride in his gifted family, goes on to say that, of the five freehold jurors acting on behalf of the village, his grandfather was the first and only classical scholar this 'dreary spot' was ever known to furnish to society. It is clear that, among so many lumbering tillers-of-the-soil, Locke felt superior, for not only was he a scholar, he also had a classical education. He adds that, when his grandfather died, he devised that his pigstrow should be passed with his farm—as if it were an important part of his heirloom.

That, as a social snapshot, is undoubtedly accurate for the first half of the eighteenth century, but changes were already beginning to overtake the place. By 1829, a hotel and several new houses had been erected, and Rutter notes that many families were resorting to Burnham for the summer. From then on Burnham's story is a familiar one of brisk Victorian development, but there was a brief interlude when it seemed that the township might splash about in the waters of prosperity.

In 1857, after the pier had been completed, ambitious projects were formulated to convert the estuary into a major dock, a station for Liverpool. Envious of Bridgwater, who was empowered to levy dues upon all shipping approaching the coast to discharge cargo between Brean and Berrow, the speculators of Burnham planned to lighten the burden of their trade. The Brean Down Scheme, after all, had lately been approved by Parliament, and Burnham, justifiably, saw herself as trembling on the threshold of a new era. But the freezing gales of reality disperse the smoke of pipe dreams. The pierhead silted up, the Harbour Scheme fell through, and, in time, even the railway traffic dwindled, and Burnham, perplexed but still intact, continued as a not-too-popular holiday resort.

* * *

The nearby prospect of Stert Island evokes no vision of buried treasure, or one-eyed rogues heaving cutlasses in mango swamps, venting obscenities at their parrots: it is dull, undramatic and rises gently above the smooth wastes of mud. Of depositional origin, mud-and-stone balls are found on the shore; swift currents roll them together and strow them about. Mushrooms, in humid weather, sprout up here as rapidly as parasols during a rainshower at Ascot. At one time this was a place where, in the season, large numbers of geese, wild duck such as wigeon, could—according to one's temperament—be shot or observed through field glasses. Now, owing to the new bird protection laws, only the latter activity is permissible. Boats are obtainable from the mainland.

The River Brue joins the Channel near Burnham after flowing almost entirely across fenland. Its name is said to be derived from 'Brw', a Celtic word meaning *swift*. This, surely, must be a joke.

At Burnham, the River Parrett also reaches the sea. From its source in

Dorsetshire, it flows in a roughly north-westerly direction to reach the Channel at Stert Point; it is navigable to Langport, a distance of 20 miles. Until 1739 it had two mouths. Then the northern one became blocked with ice, and the water was diverted into the main channel. Like the Severn, the Parrett has a bore—but it is a relatively modest one; about 18 inches usually, though a 9 feet one has been recorded. Commercially it was an important stream, too. Formerly coal, linseed oil, grain, hides, valonia, and slates were shipped up to Bridgwater and conveyed by canal to other parts; and until quite recently coastwise imports included sand, gravel, grain and tinned milk; foreign imports comprised mainly grain, fishmeal, fertiliser and timber. The large oil storage depot at Walpole owes much of its prosperity to the jetty on the Parrett. A famous local product, Bath-Brick, is manufactured out of the slime along the river's shores.

The marshes of the Parrett have historical associations, being the hiding place of Alfred the Great, at the time when his campaign against the Danish invaders was at its lowest ebb. Briefly the facts were as follows. The Danish King, Healfden, after occupying Yorkshire in A.D. 876, entered Wareham in Dorset. Alfred, ill-equipped for battle, drew up a peace treaty with him. This, however, was short-lasting, and in A.D. 878, the Danes seized Chippenham in Wiltshire. Alfred and his chiefs retreated to Athelney in Somerset and laid low in the marshes of the Parrett.

It was there, among the reedy watercourses and haunts of geese and wildfowl, that he visited the camp of the Danes disguised as a harpist, and it was there, by allowing the cakes of an elderly crone to catch fire, that he provided English history with one of its more banal episodes. The earliest traceable record of this incident was, in point of fact, written some 200 years after it was supposed to have taken place.

Alfred was, in fact, furiously active during his three months of retirement. He enlisted the natives of Somerset, Devon and Dorset to fight under his banner, threw a bridge across the Parrett, established two forts, one on an eminence near the bridge, another between Middle Zoyland and Othery, connecting and consolidating these with a long embankment. From these defences he waged guerrilla war—swooping down upon the enemy forces and withdrawing before they had time to organise themselves—harassing them with skilful sorties—priming and disciplining his army until he felt ready to face the Danes in a major engagement.

Athelney, where he founded an abbey, has a monument celebrating his refuge. William of Malmesbury, visiting it in the twelfth century, described it as almost an island and unapproachable except by boat, on account of the vast boggy tracts encircling it. In Newton Park, north-west of the abbey, the Alfred Jewel was found in 1693. This finely-wrought ornament consists of a polished gemstone, pear-shaped, tapering to the outline of a griffin, with an inscription round the edges—'AELFRED ME HEHT GEWYRCAN' (Alfred had me wrought). The setting is pure gold and contains the outline of a man seated on a throne. Now in the Oxford-based Ashmolean Museum, this pendant is thought to have been part of the handle of a book-staff.

Athelney, today, no longer qualifies as an island, but, as a result of the windings of the Parrett and the Tone, there are still a few squelchy patches to nostalgically ruminate upon. If, at some point in the future when Britain has succumbed to a European government, a warrior-patriot carries out resistance activities from this hideout, he could adopt no emblem more fitting than that of his distinguished predecessor—the red and gold dragon of Wessex.

* * *

Highbridge is rather an unloved town, an ugly sister to Burnham's none-too-glamorous Cinderella. Honeymooners shun the spot. No poet has encapsuled it in silver stanzas. No travel book urges you to see it and die, and, if it did, it would be facetiously hinting that the sight of the town would speed the process. Motorists, before the completion of the M5 motorway, recalled it as an inconvenient hold-up on the way to Bridgwater and Taunton, a traffic-jam centre, a dreary frown-town, a passing irritant in an otherwise straightforward journey.

Yet, if one thing could be said in Highbridge's favour, it would be that it is a singularly unpretentious place; it does not unfairly deceive the eye. At Weston, for instance, one sees a broad and gracious seafront, but, on tacking inland, one is abruptly confronted with narrow depressing streets and nondescript shopfronts. Like a glossy silk shirt worn over a verminous vest, it is all a bit of a cover-up; but Highbridge, being frankly and uncompromisingly drab, lures the eye with no such duplicity.

With its cheese auction, cattle market, locomotive works, timber yards, saw mills, bacon curing and brick-and-tile industries, it once knew prosperous times, and the padded-out Victorian buildings in its main street hark back to better days. When the Glastonbury Canal was revived in 1833, the lock gate at Highbridge marked its western terminus. New trade began to stir, but the advent of steam scotched this venture, and, in 1848, the canal was acquired by the Bristol and Exeter Railway Company. From this point, Highbridge flourished as a port and railhead until 1930, a date which marked the closure of the railway workshops and the subsequent decline of the town's shipping interests.

Even so, Highbridge continued to exist as a minor port, taking vessels of up to 80 tons, until late into the nineteen-forties. Today, to the industrial archaeologist, it presents scenes of interest: derelict railway yards, a narrow silt-clogged harbour, the vestiges of a canal—sights exuding the desolate patience of total neglect. Yet, for anyone interested in the growth of rail communications in the area, a study of this abandoned port is indispensable; it is the key also to Burnham's prosperity. What it lacks in looks, it makes up for in grimy integrity.

THE HOLMS

Steepholm Rising 256 feet above the racing tides of the Bristol Channel, this island was called by the Saxons, 'Steopan', or 'Reed Island'. The soil is thin and the cliffs are fissured by caves and inlets. Privet, ivy and elder manage to grow on the sandy unfruitful surface, and, of especial botanical interest, is the Peony which is indigenous. Other plants recorded growing here are Golden Samphire, Wild Cabbage, Ivy Broomrape and Rock Sea-Lavender. The presence of large and increasing Heron and Lesser Black-back Gulls has led to the establishment of a gull research station on the island. Kenneth Allsop, the conservationist and television commentator, left money in his will to the Steep Holm Trust.

A number of distinguished refugees have, in the past, used the island as a temporary hiding-place. After the Battle of Hastings, Githa, the mother of Harold Harefoot (Godwin), fled to this solitary spot. Also, the historian Gildas retired here to write the pessimistic, 'De Excidio Britanniae'. Ostensibly this was the perfect place for a studious hermit to write and meditate, but every ointment has its fly, and the learned anchorite soon found his solitude interrupted by a band of boisterous pirates. Using Steep Holm as a place to store their booty, they pillaged the nearby coast. Gildas, finding their rough manners and bawdy humour too much for his tender susceptibilities, set sail for the mainland. Glastonbury, in the vale of peace and fruitfulness, was the haven to which he finally retired, and it was there, amidst the apple orchards and gentle recluses of Avalon, he wrote and studied until death unloosed all earthly passions.

In 1320 the third Lord Berkeley built a priory here—an event chronicled in his family archives:

> This lord Maurice (1281–1326), new built the friery for the fryers and brethren in the Holmes, an Iland in Seavern and not far from his manor of Portbury.

Of this building only a few scattered bricks survive. The remains of huge gun batteries, known as the Garden, Rudder Rock, Split Rock, Summit, Laboratory and Tombstone batteries, occupy much of the island's surface. In 1825, it was recorded by John Rutter that the rabbits here have fur of a distinctly reddish cast. This point, I do not think, has been confirmed by any other authority.

Flat Holm is less precipitous than its sister island and therefore more accessible to landing by boat. It has two freshwater springs, a farmhouse which serves refreshments in summer, and a tall lighthouse (156 feet).

In 1902, the latter was the victim of a piece of cosmological slapstick: from the regions of the upper air, a shower of whitish-grey mud fell upon the lantern, plastering it like a decomposing bathing-cap. From where did it originate? A dust-shower in the Sahara was the official scientific explanation. This type of phenomena, so zealously recorded by the late Charles Fort, is not so uncommon as many people would have it—Glastonbury once experienced a downpour of frogs!

The island also had its own hermit. At the period when Gildas was on Steep Holm, Cadoc—another shadowy Celtic saint—set himself up here. Although the two anchorites never established close contact, there is a story that Cadoc presented Gildas with the gift of a bell. Contact otherwise was minimal. Gildas was perhaps too bookish and querulous for Cadoc's taste.

When fluorescent dye was introduced into certain of the underground drainage systems of the Mendips, the discoloured water was said to have re-emerged on Flat Holm. This is explicable: the island is an eroded arch of a great synclinal fold. The limestone beds of the Mendips dip under the Channel and surface at Flat Holm.

Three mounds on the turf are said to mark the graves of three of the knights who slew Thomas a Becket in Canterbury Cathedral in 1170: Reginald FitzUrse of Williton, Richard Brit of Sampford Brett and William de Tracy. It is a notable coincidence that, of the four men collectively responsible for the murder, two came from Somerset and a third also hailed from the West Country.

Although the legend of the assassins being buried here is almost certainly apocryphal, it appealed to William Bowles sufficiently to inspire him to write a sonnet on this theme and the construction of Woodspring Priory:

> These walls were built by men who did a deed
> Of blood—terrific conscience day by day,
> Followed where'er their shadow seemed to stay,
> And still, in thought, they saw their victim bleed,
> Before God's altar shrieking: pangs succeed,
> As dire upon the heart the deep sin lay,
> No tears of agony could wash away:
> Hence! to the land's remotest limits speed!
> These walls are raised in vain, as vainly flows
> Contrition's tear: Earth hide them, and thou, Sea,
> Which round the lone isle, where their bones repose,
> Dost sound for ever, their sad requiem be,

In fancy's ear, at pensive Evening's close,
Still murmuring, 'Miserere, Domine.'

In actual fact, as anyone familiar with Dean Stanley's genealogical notes will be aware, the murderers, far from being treated as outcasts from English society, were, only two years after the deed, to be seen at court on familiar terms with the king, and actually accompanying him at the chase. They were not cringing bareheaded, on their knees, in some harsh remote corner of the kingdom, but coolly pursuing their careers. De Tracy's fortunes, in particular, appears to have been unimpaired by his impetuosity—'Within four years from the murder he appears as Justiciary of Normandy; he was present at Failaise in 1174, when William, King of Scotland, did homage to Henry II, and in 1176 was succeeded in his office by the Bishop of Winchester.'

A rather eerie fragment of the island's past is seen in the ruins of the old hospital. Erected by the Cardiff Corporation towards the close of the nineteenth century, it was employed as an isolation ward for sailors with cholera and similarly devastating ailments. A crematorium is attached to it, and, in October 1900, the remains of a sailor thought to have been killed by bubonic plague were fired here.

A VICTORIAN HEALTH RESORT—GROWTH AND DECLINE

LIKE the gold rush towns of the American West, the resorts of the Somerset coast are boom towns, the product of a sudden awakening to the health-conferring benefits of exposing oneself to the embraces of gusty wet winds and chill mud-tinted waters. The extent to which Clevedon, Weston, Portishead and Burnham are of mushroom growth may be gauged by examining the summaries of the Reverend Collinson, published in 1791, and John Rutter, nearly forty years later, in 1829.

With Collinson one gets the impression that, had the work been written a hundred years earlier, his account would not have been substantially different from the one published. It is true that industrialisation had begun to affect Somerset, and details of pitheads and new farming methods indicate a certain consciousness of change, but, at the same time, his work somehow evokes a remote agricultural era.

Collinson's style, accordingly, is coarse, rambling and homely; whereas Rutter's tone is more confident, prosperous, and, to use a slightly unfair word—bourgeois. The latter is essentially, if not technically, a Victorian; his prose, befitting the age, is stately, decorous and euphemistic, and his concern over health and other matters confirms this impression. His work, significantly, left the presses when George Stephenson had just developed 'The Rocket'; Collinson's in the year the radical, Thomas Paine, published his 'Rights of Man'.

Collinson's massive work treats each parish more or less individually, giving a brief account of the topography of the district, cryptically outlining the settlement pattern, and following this with a more detailed description of the manor house and parish church. References to other buildings are noticeably terse and tend to be brisk references to groups of 'cottage dwellings' clustering around the spring-line of a hill or adjoining the church.

Rutter's study is, however, strikingly different; it chronicles the changes that are overcoming the area. Descriptions of 'handsome' new hotels being erected, of medicinal baths, roads, piers and footpaths, confirm that much has taken place in the period separating the publication of the two works.

He was, of course, writing on the eve of a period of truly phenomenal growth. In 1837, Britain's population was around 26,000,000 with 1,250,000 British abroad in the colonies; by 1897, it had risen to almost 40,000,000, with over 10,000,000 more British abroad expanding the Empire.

This situation was also being reflected, to a lesser extent, in the West Country. Somerset was relatively remote from the big centres of industry, but its statistics still reflect this general flowering of people and trade. In 1821, Weston-super-Mare's population was 738, comprising 147 families living in 126 houses, compared with 8,033 in 1861 and 12,872 in 1881. This is spectacular growth by any standards. Clevedon's population, at the time of the census in 1801, was 334; it then rose rapidly from 1,147 in 1831 to 4,091 in 1871. Burnham also enjoyed a measure of popularity showing an increase of over a thousand in two decades; and Portishead, taking initiative from Bristol Corporation's entrepreneurial interest in its development as a dock and watering-place, grew steadily from 800 in 1831 to 3,064 in 1881.

One of the reasons accounting for this burgeoning of seaside towns was health. Throughout the century, new discoveries were being made concerning the spread of infectious diseases, the growth of germ viruses, the importance of properly filtered drinking water, the invigorating properties of salt water and sea breezes, and prosperous business men, learning of these benefits, started building weekend residences on the coast, so that they might have somewhere to recuperate after sojourning in industrial centres as far apart as Birmingham and Dundee.

Fashion was also a major factor. Spas and inland resorts, like Tunbridge and Cheltenham, were beginning to lose their vogue, and, by degrees, their indolent habituees started to migrate towards the coast. In actual fact, the first real town to gain resort status had been Scarborough in the mid-eighteenth century. Lyme Regis, Weymouth and Brighton followed in its wake. George IV, notably, conferred distinction on the latter by being regularly seen strutting down the promenade with an arm around one of his minister's necks. Close to the Capital, soon to be favoured with a fantastic Oriental pavilion, it fast acquired the reputation of a Bath-beside-the-sea, and the glittering rows of stuccoed residences increased yearly. In much the same way—and over the same period of time—Clevedon, Weston and Portishead, by virtue of their proximity to Bath and Bristol, became fashionable watering-places, and it was to be popularly proclaimed that Weston's relationship to Bristol was akin to Brighton and London.

But naturally this boom was not isolated from other causes. Economic and social factors were also contributory. For instance, it was an outstandingly prosperous period economically: the star of the British Empire was still firmly in ascendance; foreign trade was flourishing; home industry was lining the pockets of the commercial classes; railways were sprouting fresh tentacles throughout the kingdom; cheap transport was being made available to the masses, and money—if nowhere evenly distributed—was abundant. By the mid-nineteenth century, a quarter of the world's trade was handled by British ports, and over a third of the world's traded commodities found their origin in British mines, mills, factories and workshops.

In this atmosphere, the seaside resorts germinated. After a tentative start around 1820, the notion of a day beside the sea blossomed into an obsession. Some thirty years later, a behavioural pattern had been established, and children were to be seen on beaches everywhere, burying their papas in sand, slinging oozy clots of mud at one another, uprooting the homes of slumbering crabs, and gleefully cavorting with simple unspoilt Lord-of-the-Flies naturalness. The sight of them thus disporting themselves warmed the hearts of parents and sightseers alike, and inspired guidebook hacks to adopt a style of copywriter's mandarin:

> The sands are a never-failing source of amusement to children, and in the height of the season they may be seen there by the thousand, armed with bucket and spade, busily engaged in the erection of battlemented fortress or turreted tower, or in the excavation of miniature ravines and trenches; or, it may be that you will see them with a more aquatic turn of mind shoeless and stockingless wading through the cool refreshing wavelets which in fine weather flow into the bay so gently that all sense of danger is dispelled.

The new craze could have been said to represent an abrupt about turn in attitudes to water in general. The association of pleasure with that vast mass of liquescent salt engirdling these islands was hitherto unknown. Formerly, the sea had been looked upon as the epitome of ruthlessness and terror, Kipling's old grey widow-maker—a remorseless devourer of ships and men:

> That night I saw ten thousand bones
> Coffined in ships, in weeds and stones;
> Saw how the Sea's strong jaws could take
> Big iron ships like rats to shake . . .

It is no coincidence that the modern hotels of all well-known resorts inevitably face the sea, implying there is pleasure in observing its varying moods, but that often the old fishermen's cottages have their back turned to the foreshore. They were built before a courtship with the green earth-shaker had ever been contemplated.

Equally significant were the natives of these resorts. In their own way, they too contributed to the pleasure of the early tourist. Back in the Georgian heyday, manual labour had been regarded somewhat disdainfully; it was something crude and utilitarian that offended polite eyeballs, but, with the extension of transport facilities, the middle classes were able to have the opportunity of observing the coastal dwellers going about their everyday toil. The fishermen of England, whose way of life so dramatically differed from the residents of the fashionable spas and commercial centres, radiated something of the aura that the Laplanders retain to this day. Not only were they men who provided an important edible commodity, they were also part of the necessary window-display of any resort.

At Birnbeck, for instance, before the pier was erected, a narrow causeway of stones, covered at high tide, linked the islet with the mainland. The fishermen of Weston, some of whom were aged ninety, would stake out their nets here, and, after the tide had retreated, return on donkeys and ponies to gather their spoils. In the sprat and herring season, the scene at this spot was an animated one. Jobbers, keen to barter with the fisherman, would group themselves around the stands, and children, carrying baskets, would eagerly glean any stray sliver of wriggling silver that escaped from the nets. Such spectacles were relished by early holidaymakers; after the clammy pump-rooms and dehydrated gossip of Harrogate and Cheltenham, they smacked of newness and raw vigorous life.

And, in rough weather, snug in capes and shawls, they could safely watch the dangers besetting local mariners trying to dock their boats or negotiate a headland. From the cast-iron security of a new-made pier, they could observe fragile craft heeling and bucking and seas creaming over the bows of barques and trawlers. They could derive the elementary satisfaction of experiencing danger without feeling actually threatened by it—participation combined with emotional detachment. To see men pitting their lives against the most savage and untempered of elements was an entirely new experience to pampered Victorian gentlewomen, and one, no doubt, that made the attractions of inland retreats seem by comparison small beer indeed.

Less typically, the sea also provided some Victorian minds of vertiginously high elevation with titbits of moral instruction. An early writer, watching the surf advance and retreat on Burnham's smooth and stone-free shore, immediately hit on a profound ethical parallel:

> It is a singular but undeniable fact that the restless sea, which overcomes and wears away the opposing, and apparently irresistible cliffs and rocks, and which breaks down the strongest artificial barriers, recedes of its own accord from flat and unopposing shores. It overcomes an imposing bulwark, it is in its turn overcome by the passive resistance of an unopposing strand. There is in fact a perfect harmony between the natural and the moral world—opposition creates opposition—gentleness is often of greater avail than strength—passive forbearance a more sure defence than the most powerful aggressive weapon. Scripture reminds us of the same truth, in the proverb that 'a mild answer turneth away wrath.'

Such passages, the more affected of which would qualify for entry in Private Eye's 'Pseud's Corner', are common fare in nineteenth-century tourist handbooks. The comparisons and homilies are, admittedly, in many cases, a little strained, but it is still possible to admire their dogged ingenuity and unrelieved sobriety of tone. Nothing in the way of this post-Wordsworthian fall-out crops up in contemporary tourist guides, which stick tenaciously to hotels and food, but at least one modern poet—W. H. Auden—attempted to use landscape to similar ends.

Some resorts were almost ostentatiously eligible for patronage, but the Somerset resorts, though salubrious, did not all have particularly attractive settings. Weston, in particular, sited on a huge raw arc of a bay, was exposed to fierce winds and backed by miles of drear moorland. Burnham, similarly, was a rather uncouth-looking place confined among bleak sandy waste land. Yet both of these resorts could at least boast fine sandy beaches, while Portishead and Clevedon, although finely-situated in hilly glades, could only display expanses of clicking shingle.

As regards these resorts then, the health factor was undoubtedly crucial. There was a new novelty in the discovery that certain types of air and climate could benefit one's physical and mental wellbeing, and it is noticeable that nearly all the guidebooks to this region have separate sections dealing often extensively with these matters. Different resorts, it would seem, had different specialities. Weston guides inevitably refer to the gaseous vapour popularly known as 'ozone' exuded by their local mud; this exhalation, it was claimed, contained iodine, bromine and other 'nerve-restoring' and 'curative' chemicals. Burnham and Clevedon took an equal pride in their mud and endowed it with identical properties. It seems that, in lieu of a blue sea and royal patronage, the Somerset resorts decided to play up the health side.

Each resort had its own resident physician, who, at fairly frequent intervals, would issue statements concerning such matters. Dr Benjamin Ward, a noted writer on matters of hygiene was resident at Clevedon for a month, and stated in a lecture that there was no other place where he had sojourned which came so near to his idea as a 'city of health'. He added that the air was singularly adapted to those engaged in literary work and that the drinking water was also of good quality.

Burnham also found a good promoter in the person of Dr Hemming, reputed physician, author of 'An historical account of the medicinal waters or springs of Daviesville, at Burnham'—a work which, on account of its title alone, was never doomed to titillate the appetites of thousands of readers.

Weston, as far as such matters were concerned, had more than its fair share of attention. The Reverend Jackson, author of an excellent guidebook, wrote about the town's healthful qualities with true fervour. 'Weston winds,' he proclaimed, 'are known all over Somerset.' He then cited the example of Earl Eldon, who, when nerve and bodily vigour failed him, was urged by his physician to make carriage journeys of many miles per day, so that he might be injected with new life by being blown upon by long columns of air. And, of course, Weston, if it could boast little else in those days, was certainly blessed with these.

Local drinking water and springs also received minute analysis. The Reverend Jackson solemnly wrote that no pains could be better bestowed than in learning the exact qualities of the drinking water consumed at any place of health resort. Even more gravely he adds a footnote to the effect that, should filtering be ever deemed advisable at Weston, no device would be more suitable to the water than 'Bischof's Spongy Iron Filter'.

Jackson, trying to account for Weston's excessive salubruity, even goes so far as to invoke science—'The bay at Weston forms at low water a large evaporating pan, bottomed by a kind of clayey lias, which, when burned, has the property of setting under, and is known in the district as "brown lime.".' Then, uncertain as to what all this exactly amounts to, he evades making a pertinent conclusion and takes refuge in humour—'Whatever may be the particular chemicals thrown into the air, there can be no doubt that, to speak Theodore-Hookianly, they contribute certain strong "sniffs of the briny".'

Yet science was prepared to rush in where clergymen fear to tread, and, from no less impeccable an authority than Sir Humphry Davy, the Bethlehem star of the mineshafts, we are given the penultimate explanation for Weston's excessive healthfulness—'The salubruity of the south-west winds can be attributed to the large portions of oxygen they imbibe in passing over the vast vegetation of the extensive plains of the Savannahs of South America.'

Mortality rates were also cited in these arguments. For instance, it was a much-quoted fact that, according to the Medical Officer of Health for the district, Dr Pizey, Clevedon's mortality rate for 1883 was 12·34 per 1,000 or about half the average rate for the United Kingdom. Weston, similarly, had its promoter in an anonymous gentleman who called himself 'Health'. He wrote a studious and detailed letter to the 'Weston Mercury', of January 27th, 1872, pointing out how one was less likely to die in Weston, whose water, deriving from limestone, was hard, than in towns supplied with soft water. Quoting the distinguished Dr Letheby, who had recently given evidence before the Commons for the 'Edinburgh and District Water Bill', he presented these statistics—'Average death-rate per 1000, hard water supply, 22·00; average death-rate per 1000, soft water supply, 28·04; death-rate in England at the same time, 22·68.'

Nor were local drainage schemes ignored. Guidebooks often contain recondite expertise concerning the intercepting tanks, valve flaps and the various outfalls of the local sewerage systems. Weston, again, excels in this particular area, being one of the first towns to be fitted with a special ventilation system whereby sewer gas, by being released into the upper air, was rendered innocuous.

The seaside also sparked off a minor manufacturing industry of health products, particularly of the aerated-salts-and-water type. For instance, Ross and Co, of Weston, proudly advertised their 'Soda, Seltzer, Potash, & Quinine Waters', all bottles of which were well charged with carbonic gas and had been previously submitted to the public analyst and pronounced free from metallic and other impurities. Another local product was Griffith's 'Essence of Sea-Weed', a truly—if we are to take its advertising at face value—amazing product:

Certainly the solution would seem to be an extraordinary versatile one, capable of curing anything, except perhaps a broken leg. Where modern copywriters tend to promote multiple products for single specific purposes, the Victorians declared their items to be almost fantastically versatile. In fact, a sick man reading about Griffith's 'essence' might justifiably feel that a product which is so broad and all-encompassing in the range of maladies which it is capable of counteracting, is finally not particularly effective against anything, which, regretfully, was probably the case. It is also notable that it is promoted as an 'Internal Remedy', and this is fairly typical, the Victorians being enthusiastic swallowers of bizarre concoctions in their relentless Odyssey after the hale and hearty God of health. So rapt were they on this single-minded quest that it was once customary to swallow sea-water,

C. GRIFFITH,

Dispensing and Family Chemist,

35, HIGH STREET, WESTON-SUPER-MARE.

Quality, not Price being the primary consideration in the Purchase of Drugs and Chemicals, reliance may be confidently placed in this Establishment.

GRIFFITH'S

ESSENCE OF SEA-WEED,

For Spinal Affections, Rheumatism, Sprains, Bruises, Lumbago, Swellings of the Glands, Chilblains, Stiffness of the Joints, Tumours, Weakness of the Limbs, Scrofula, &c.

C. GRIFFITH introduced this Essence to the notice of the public in 1856. It contains all the virtues of the Sea-weed, will keep any length of time, and is strongly recommended as an External Remedy for Stiffness or Wea'ness in the Joints, Relaxation of the Ligaments and Tendons, Contractions, Stiffness, and General Rigidity, Deformities in the Joints or Limbs of Ricketty, Scrofulous or badly-nursed Children, Weakness of the Spine, Rheumatism, Rheumatic Gout, and Lumbago. It disperses Swellings and Strengthens the Joints injured by recent Sprains and other Accidents. It is a perfect cure for Chilblains, quickly relieving the itching and reducing the swelling. It reduces Tumours and Swelling of the Glands. As an Internal Remedy it is recommended for Scrofula, or King's Evil and General Weakness. For Rheumatism, Lumbago, Goitre, Bronchocele, and Swellings of the Glands, it is advised to administer it internally during the external application, as it greatly assists in the cure. Numerous testimonials of its efficacy are being continually received.

This Essence is prepared only by C. GRIFFITH, Pharmaceutical Chemist, High Street, Weston-super-Mare. Sold in Bottles, 1s. 1½d., 2s. 9d., and 4s. 6d. Wholesale Agents: Barclay, Edwards, and Sanger, London. Be sure to ask for Griffith's Essence of Sea-weed, and observe the Trade Mark.

---

in the belief that it cleansed the intestines and stimulated the circulation. It is doubtful, however, whether this practice ever caught on to a large extent at Portishead, Clevedon, Weston-super-Mare or Burnham, as the colour and sedimentary deposits contained in the waves that washed these particular townships were not calculated to quicken the thirst.

To itemise all these aspects of each resort would be unnecessarily tedious, but to ignore them would also be unsatisfactory, because health was a seminal factor relating to the birth and development of many coastal retreats.

This led to a number of inaccuracies being occasionally perpetrated. For instance, the climate of specific resorts is presented along the following lines. Weston is a town whose air has a peculiar 'dryness', the temperature being mild without being relaxing, and effective for reviving sufferers from 'mental and physical exhaustion'. Clevedon is so dry and clear, so free from humidity, that it is specially recommended for pulmonary complaints and sufferers from rheumatism or dyspepsia, as well as convalescents from fever. Either the climate of the area has changed dramatically over the last century or else the authors of certain guidebooks are guilty of a degree of self-deception.

Of the illnesses that these resorts were alleged to cure, apart from the ones listed previously, one can say little. In the main, they tended to be hazily-defined psychosomatic complaints, the symptoms of which were boredom, flagging energy and attacks of spiritual weariness—emotions of a type experienced by many folk during a party-political boradcast or browsing through a student rag magazine.

Furthermore one finds oneself compelled to ask—What rendered the Victorians so prone to 'mental and physical exhaustion'? Could it have been attending lectures by Dr Benjamin Ward on such topics as 'The Chemo-Therapeutic Benefits to be derived from a stay at Clevedon, Somersetshire', or reading booklets entitled 'An historical account of the medicinal waters or springs of Daviesville, Burnham'?

Yet, finally, from all the waffly eulogies to health, from all the earnest statistics and discourses on sea breezes, it is possible to extract a terse and honest message, the general gist of which would run—'Fresh air, swimming and moderate exercise is beneficial.'

Entertainments, initially, were considered subsidiary to health considerations, but they still compare reasonably with the contemporary scene. The diversions offered at Clevedon around 1880 included lawn tennis, croquet, boating and donkey riding on the beach, and once a week a train service operated enabling an inhabitant of the town to be conveyed to and from the Theatre, in Park Row, or a concert at the Colston Hall for less than a sum a resident at Clifton or Redland would have to pay for a cab. The normal return fare to Bristol at that time was only one shilling, and, for a further sixpence, it was possible to negotiate with the Tramway Company a lift to and from the hall or theatre.

In the season, music never seems to have been lacking, and Weston employed a very professional group of musicians, 'The Rhine Band', who resided so long at the town that they came to be thought of as naturalised 'Westonians'. Clevedon also had a creditable band, the company of which gave concerts upon the pier and at various points in the town. Portishead, at this period, offered fewer tourist enticements. Her visitors could stroll round the headland and visit the *Formidable*, anchored 400 yards off the pier, or ascend the numerous wooded footpaths; if they were less energetically inclined, they might be able to drum up a game of billiards at the Royal Hotel. Burnham's attractions were equally limited; briefly, they consisted of two puzzle gardens, the acreage of which were so small, that, only if a visitor entered them blindfold at midnight, would he stand the remotest chance of getting lost.

Not everybody, human nature being unvarying, delighted in such innocent pleasures. There were some young spruces, in particular, who preferred more predatory pursuits. A visitor to Clevedon in 1865 wrote—'At a certain quiet watering-place, not sixteen miles from Bristol, two *creatures*—I cannot call them men, fresh from the hands of the tailor and hairdresser, find a certain undefinable sort of pleasure in *prowling* about the public walks, and insolently accosting every female that crosses their path.'

It is stating the obvious to draw attention to the fact that things have dramatically changed since those days. People no longer, before selecting a place to spend their holidays, read earnestly-worded pamphlets outlining each individual resort's health speciality. The chemical constituents of the water they drink, the bracingness of the air they breathe, the salty refreshingness of the waves they swim in—all this is old hat.

Today, as a visit to Weston-super-Mare will confirm, a seaside town is expected to be a microcosm of a city: restaurants, funfairs, cinemas, bowling alleys, ice rinks and nightclubs are now part of the seaside scene. Health is no longer a draw. Entertainment, above all, is the primary factor determining a resort's prosperity, unless, of course, as is the case with the Cornish and Devon villages, the surrounding landscape is of exceptional natural beauty.

In this atmosphere, Weston-super-Mare, the best situated of the Channel watering-places for expansion, continued to develop, while Portishead became increasingly industrialised. Burnham still contrived to exist as a convenient retreat for the inhabitants of Bridgwater, its salt air providing an exciting contrast to the effluvia produced by the cellophane factory. As for Clevedon, its reputation dwindled over the years, and it became an occasional place resorted to by day-trippers for 'peace and quiet'. The buildings and the people remain, but the obsessions accounting for its present-day appearance have evaporated.

FOUR GEOLOGICAL SITES

BATTERY POINT
Compact sandstones, conglomerates and marls lie in unconformity upon Black Nore Sandstone. Fossils are plentiful: red limestone crammed with crinoids, bryzoa and small gastropods. At the south end of the Portishead Parade, the Woodhill Bay Fish Bed contains scales of Glyptopomus, Holoptychius and other species.

MIDDLE HOPE
As at Spring Cove, Carboniferous Limestone is interbedded with tuffs. The limestone is, however, more richly fossiliferous: bivalves, gastropods and crinoids. The igneous rocks, too, are veined with calcareous material. At Swallow Cliff, there is a notable Raised Beach with sand, shells and mollusca.

SPRING COVE

Red olivine-basalt is exposed in a striking cliff-face. Of volcanic origin, it was probably poured out of the sea-bottom from nearby vents during the lower Carboniferous Period. At the eastern extremity of the outcrop Amygdaloids occur frequently in the basalt. A Raised Beach is also identifiable.

BREAN DOWN

This was an island about a 1000 years ago rising above the reed-swamps and saltings. The Down itself is Carboniferous Limestone. From the south side of the cliff a fascinating geological succession has been mapped, down through grey-green stony clay and Iron and Bronze Age potsherds, to the bones of Reindeer, Bison and Arctic Fox. In the Quarry below Uphill church are three small caves, one of which has yielded the bones of 23 species of mammals, palaeolithic flints and human skulls.

VISITOR'S CRITICISMS

The coastal belt is popular among tourists. In and about Weston, some 350,000 people spent sums ranging from £6 to £9 million yearly from 1965 onwards. The area has also been criticised by holidaymakers. They have complained of misleading advertisements displaying golden sand and a cerulean sea; of the litter washed up on the shore or left lying around by other visitors; of the poor road access to certain parts of the region; of encountering untreated sewage during their afternoon swims; of the presence of two mountainous refuse tips along the coast; of the lack of evening entertainment facilities in places like Burnham, Clevedon and Portishead; of the shortage of good restaurants and cafes. Yet these criticisms are levelled at many resorts, both in England and abroad, and should not be regarded as outright condemnations of a particular area.

SUMMARY 1.
THE MENDIP HILLS

THE Mendip Hills—like a massive green tidal wave—rise steeply above the Somerset Plain. Gently undulating, treeless, stabbed with caves and swallet holes, incised with deep ravines, they exhibit the typical features of karst. Economically from earliest times they have been of primary importance: lead and zinc were the principal ores mined, but quantities of manganese were also worked in the Dolomitic Conglomerate of the hills around East Harptree. The industry, after reaching its peak between 1628 and 1659, declined sharply. The surface lodes had been exhausted and the technology necessary to pump the deeper mines free of water was not available. Mining on a large scale ceased. The land surface was left, pocked, irregular and pimpled with slagheaps.

The first developers of the mines on a large scale, however, were the Romans. They established a large lead-mining settlement at Charterhouse. This hamlet, set among the 'gruffy-grounds' (old filled-in mineshafts), is near Blackdown (1,067 feet), the highest point on the Mendips. Little else can be said of this community, except that its name derives from a long-vanished Carthusian priory. Priddy, four miles to the south-east, is slightly larger and has a pleasant inn which breeds racing snails. Outside the village are a group of Hut Circles and Nine Barrows: nine remarkable humps of earth rumoured to be the graves of tribal chiefs. Priddy Pool, a reedy sheet of water, is said to be bottomless and provides the melancholy-minded with the romantic opportunity of drowning throughout eternity.

The most visited features of the Mendips are the dry gorges, the northernmost example of which may be seen at Burrington Combe. The Rev. Augustus Toplady, whilst sheltering during a storm here, was moved to write the hymn 'Rock of Ages'. The defile is narrow, winding and fissured with caves. Dolebury Camp, adjoining, is an impressively-situated Iron Age earthwork. Brockley Combe, another limestone cleft, is also close at hand. 'It is a fine romantic glen', wrote John Rutter, 'more than a mile in length, and very narrow, each being a steep cliff of transcendent richness and beauty. The crags resemble ruins and every fissure of the rocks affords an asylum for vegetation, which springs vigorously from them, and shades the surface cover with mosses of the richest tints.' The combe is also haunted: a phantom stagecoach, from time to time, drives down it, and it is also visited by the apparition of an old lady—probably Diana Swan, the guardian priestess of the glen, who used to serve refreshments from her cottage at the entrance to the glade. She, or some other elderly crone who lived nearby, is said to have been brutally murdered.

Goblin Combe, near Cleeve, is possibly the quietest and most spellbinding of these limestone ravines. Silent, green and ghostly, tall frost-cracked pinnacles rear up on the north side of the enclave: Cleve Toot—a huge skull-like hump of fractured rock—is the most commanding of these. At the end of the gorge are the remains of an ancient volcano: difficult to locate—even for a geologist.

Yet the most spectacular—if the most desecrated—dry gorge is at Cheddar. This, despite touristic accretions, should be seen. The lower part of the defile has suffered worst from commercialisation: neon-lit grottoes, ugly cafes, souvenir stalls, squadrons of cars, metal litter baskets, and the stream tidily walled-up by the water board. Nevertheless, it is the nearest approach to a canyon England has got, and the emerald foliage clinging to the scarred and shattered limestone battlements in the upper gorge is deeply impressive.

Axbridge, a few miles away, also has much to offer: King John's Hunting Lodge, an interesting Museum, and the church of Saint John the Baptist, a cruciform edifice in the Decorated and Perpendicular styles. John Naish, the fashionable eighteenth-century miniaturist who studied under Joshua Reynolds, was a native of Axbridge.

The whole area is rich in wild flowers: the Cheddar Pink, a delicate sweetly-scented flower, grows to a height of 8 inches and blooms in June and July; also, the Spring Cinquefoil, flowering on the rocky slopes behind Axbridge, the Alpine Pennycress, sprouting beside the tumps and decaying mineshafts, the Bloody Cranesbill and many others.

SUMMARY 2.

EXMOOR, THE BRENDON, QUANTOCK AND BLACKDOWN HILLS

THIS upland area, heathery and stag-infested, has inspired many pens: R. D. Blackmore, Eric Delderfield and John Davidson. The northward-flowing streams of the moor have carved huge trenches in the Old Red Sandstone producing awesome coastal scenery: tiny roads climbing massive and blunt-nosed cliffs and descending into steamy and thickly-vegetated glens—see Lynton and Lynmouth. Inland, the landscape is softer and more cultivated than that of Dartmoor. The hills are covered with buff-green grass and support herds of stags, native ponies, red Devon cattle, flocks of Exmoor Horn and Scottish Blackface sheep. The uplands reach their greatest altitude at Dunkery Beacon, a lofty purple dome presiding over the Exe valley, with views extending to Brown Willy on Bodmin Moor and the khaki ramparts of Yes Tor and Cawsand Beacon. To the west are The Chains, a wide boggy plateau, the spongy soil of which feeds the sources of many rivers. Apart from the churches, the architecture of the area is stolidly functional: cob cottages, thick-walled farmhouses and the occasional Georgian or Victorian mansion. Prehistoric remnants, though thinly scattered, are present, notably at Cow Castle and Mounsey Castle. The most famous of these antique engineering projects, however, is the Tarr Steps, a large clapper bridge, built out of 5-ton stone slabs and thought to be over 2,500 years old. This considerable structural feat crosses the River Barle, the damned headwaters of which form Pinkworthy Pond: a grim puddle built by John Knight for reasons unknown or forgotten. A young farm labourer, after being jilted by a barmaid, drowned himself in these glum un-Mediterranean waters.

Adjoining Exmoor, relatively unspoilt, and swelling magnificently above the cattle-rich vale of Taunton Deane, are the Brendon Hills, rising to 1,390 feet and sporting on their lower slopes Willet's Tower—a staggering ruin falling within the parish of Elworthy. Nettlecombe Church, folded away among these stag and fox-hunting parts, has a lovely font, some fifteenth-century heraldic glass and a priceless chalice of the same period.

To the south, in the heart of the cider country, the Blackdown Hills rise to a height of 1,035 feet at Staple Hill. The villages here, too, have their points of interest: Wellington, on a hill $2\frac{1}{2}$ miles south of the town, has a monument to the Iron Duke himself: a stark stone bayonet, 175 feet high, and affording excellent views; Churchstanton, on the Devonshire border, has seven large and well-stocked fishponds and a church notable for its intricate window tracery, while Corfe, in memory of its citizens who sacrificed themselves in the Great War, adorns its churchyard with a large Celtic Cross, and Buckland St Mary, more eccentrically, displays a group of flint cairns called Robin Hood's Rues and an earthwork named Castle Neroche.

The Quantock Hills, dainty and compact, offer similar attractions to Exmoor: stags, wild ponies, heather, yokel cottages and deep green clefts slit by tinkling streams. The village of Broomfield, however, was the birthplace of Andrew Crosse, pioneer electrician and modern Prometheus. He made great stir in the nineteenth century when he gave details of an experiment which produced living insects. His home, Fyne Court, can still be seen, but his laboratory was destroyed by fire; the bench on which he conducted numerous experiments is preserved in the parish church. Crosse, in his researches, made use of the nearby Holwell Cavern, geologically complex, displaying brilliant and fragile crystal formations.

AN ALPHABETICAL LIST OF FOLLIES, ODDITIES, ECCENTRICITIES, PLACES TO VISIT, ETC., PLUS HISTORICAL, TOPOGRAPHICAL AND ANECDOTAL MISCELLANEA

Ashill. From this parish sprung John Hanning Speke (1827–64), the explorer who discovered the source of the Nile and accompanied Sir Richard Burton in his journey to Central Africa. He met his death as a result of a shooting accident. The Church of St Andrew at Dowlish Wake, where he is buried, has a memorial window and monument to him. Capland, nearby, has a Chalybeate Spring.

Banwell. This village, mentioned by Leland in his 'Itinerary', is crammed with features of antiquarian interest: the Court House—formerly Bishop Beckington's ancient hall and built on the site of a Saxon monastery; St Andrew's Church, in the Decorated style, with its lofty pinnacled tower and richly-carved oak screen; Banwell Castle, built in the Tudor style, and the nearby Roman remains and hill forts. Yet possibly the most stylish—and fast-disappearing—feature of the parish is the former Estate of Bishop Law. Laid out with grottoes, towers, gothic arches, medieval carvings, pediments, pyramids and neatly-scanning verse inscriptions, this was once a superbly state-managed scenic walk. The name 'Banwell' is partly derived from a spring in the centre of the village which yields up to 12 tons of water per minute and has never been known to dry up. It has, however, been effectively concealed by the water board.

Barrow Gurney. Reservoirs, fed from springs at the foot of the Mendips, are situated at the height of 310 feet in this parish. Their 750 million gallons helps to slake the thirst of Bristol. On the present site of Barrow Court, the Barrow Minchin Priory of Benedictine Nuns was founded by Eva de Gourney in 1212 and suppressed in 1536. The Elizabethan mansion, containing elegant stucco ceilings and carved chimney-pieces, has attached to its grounds a tithe barn (now a gymnasium) with a high-pitched roof. Around 1800, a woman's headless body was found concealed beneath the central hearthstone. Still later, in the garden, the head was discovered. The most feasible explanation of this macabre phenomena must lie in the ancient custom of burying horses, dogs, cats, or even parts of humans, under the main fireplace of the house, in the belief that it will promote domestic calm and stability. It is preferable, however, that the person concerned has died a 'natural' death before one undertakes such forms of concealment.

Bath. Rated as the best-planned in Britain, this town has a warm Roman bath, fine Georgian architecture and a traffic problem. Lansdown Cemetery, on a hill overlooking the settlement, exhibits the Tomb of William Beckford, millionaire-eccentric, brilliant letter writer, white elephant collector, novelist and tower-builder extraordinary. This sombre, once structurally unstable monument, built in the Italian style with a 130 feet tower, encloses a sarcophagus, designed by Mr Beckford himself, containing his interred remains. It is his one monument—apart from 'Vathek'—which survives to this day. But the city's most appreciated features are its wheat-coloured terraces and architectural masterworks like Royal Crescent, a group of self-contained dwellings integrated to form a palatial whole. Interesting in an eye-catching sort of way, is Ralph Allen's Sham Castle (1762). This edifice looks almost too determinedly like what its meant to represent.

Bathford. This village, over five miles long and situated on the banks of the Avon, has two Roman villas, burial mounds and a square tapering tower, built in 1840 for Mr Wade Brown and accordingly called Brown's Folly. The ancient bridge which fords the river was once part of the Roman 'Fosseway'.

Beckington. On the Frome–Bath road is the Sebright Stone, a Witenagemot stone, formerly marking the meeting-place of the supreme Anglo-Saxon council; also, the boundary between Somerset and Wiltshire.

Beechbarrow Farm. On the Wells–Bristol road, there is a remarkable and ambitious sculpture. Upheld by four tall concrete piers, it is a powerful representation of Romulus and Remus being suckled by the she-wolf. The artist, Gaetano Celestra, was an Italian prisoner of war. In the field behind the sculpture are the old sheds and nissen huts of the P.O.W. camp.

Blagdon. Among the gentle corrugations of the Mendip Hills, the tiny artificial lake of Blagdon glistens, like a fragment of blue glass on a rumpled billiard cloth. Some of Britain's finest trout fishing is to be had on its waters. The village itself, with its whitewashed cottages and Perpendicular church of Dolomitic Conglomerate, is also attractive—though it's rapidly becoming a dormitory for Bristol! Not far away is Rickford Glen, one of the most fairytale spots in Somerset. Another reservoir, Chew Valley Lake, lies about two miles east of Blagdon. This slightly glum expanse, drowning a Roman road and villa, is popular among picnickers and has boating and fishing facilities.

Bridgwater. This municipal borough and seaport was used by the Duke of Monmouth as his headquarters before the Battle of Sedgemoor (1685) and is the birthplace of Admiral Blake. There is Georgian architecture in Castle Street. John Hillaby, master walker, remarked on the Flemish atmosphere around the Parrett's banks. Brassieres are manufactured here.

Bristol. This city, the handsomest of the provincial metropolises, has a Zoo with white tigers, the finest parish church in Britain (St Mary's Redcliffe), the first large propeller-driven iron ship (Brunel's SS Great Britain), one of the most elegant suspension bridges in the world (Clifton Bridge), and some 160 parks scattered about its 26,345 acres. Goldeney House, a superb Gothic folly, merits a visit, as do the Christmas Steps, one of the oldest streets in the city, dating from the first half of the seventeenth century. Also worth viewing is the foot of the Avon Gorge. There climbers, looking small as flies, peg their way across wide exposed slabs of limestone while lorries scuttle like bugs beneath them. Berkeley, just outside the city, has what is probably the oldest inhabited Castle in Britain. Edward II met his end there after the administration of a ghastly enema.

Burrow Bridge. On the summit of a hill locally dubbed as 'The Mump', overlooking the Parrett, are the remains of a thirteenth-century church, onto which bits of eighteenth-century Gothic have been grafted.

Butleigh Wootton. On the summit of a hill 327 feet high is the Hood Memorial Column, a 110 feet pillar commemorating Vice-Admiral Sir Samuel Hood, commander-in-chief of the fleet in the East Indies, who died at Madras on December 24th, 1814.

Castle Cary. The Round House, near the town centre, was formerly used as a lock-up. Outside the town, four thick pillars mark the foundations of the ancient Castle. Nearby the tiny River Cary rises.

Chard. This ancient borough and market town, formerly called 'Cerde' after Cedric, King of the West Saxons, has adopted a striking design for its mayoral chain: two medieval peacocks with foliated sprays in the centre, enclosed by medallions and shields, one of which is emblazoned with the arms of Edward I. The Town Hall, a chaste Classical building with a cupola, stands on the site of an earlier Gothic fabric. The town has long associations with the cloth and lace industry.

Chew Magna. Good Late Medieval and eighteenth-century architecture enliven the aspect of this village: Chew Court, with its Tudor gateway and tower dating from Henry VII's reign; Harford House, displaying stepped window lintels; and the Pelican Inn, sashed, gabled and socially vital. Of equal interest is St Andrew's church, housing a painted oak effigy of a knight of the de Hautville family; and, for folly fanciers, there is Chew Tower, short and cobbly, in grey and white stone, and snuggling at the bottom of a reservoir.

Christon. In the Lox Yeo valley, the church here is celebrated for its architectural simplicity and fine setting. 'No one,' writes Arthur Mee, 'who has seen this porch, framing in its arch this perfect Norman doorway, can forget it. There are few who will not accept the invitation of the ancient stone seats to stay awhile by this rough horseshoe arch, those lovely mouldings, and look out at the other picture in the frame, where Crook's Peak shoots up like a miniature volcano from the Mendip ridge.'

Claverton. On the Bath–Warminster road, the parish church contains the pyramidal tomb of Ralph Allen Esq., patron of Henry Fielding, who immortalised him as Squire Allworthy in 'Tom Jones'. A flight of stone steps behind the church formerly led to the ancient manor house and were the scene of a violent scuffle in the Civil War. Hampton Camp, north of the village, is bounded by a dyke and a cliff.

Cleeve Abbey. William de Roumara, Earl of Lincoln, founded this Cistercian house at the end of the twelfth century. The cloisters are, in the main, still intact: a pleasant shadowy stroll among arches and collonades.

Cothelstone'. St Agnes' Well, near the manor house, is an ancient foundation, spotted with rosettes of yellow and green lichen and protected by a stone canopy. Nearby, on one of the hill summits, is a ruined tower (Cothelstone Beacon), affording views over eleven counties.

Crook's Peak. A limb of the Mendips, this tawny-brown hill is the Matterhorn of N.W. Somerset. Quarrying operations have bitten and chewed its flanks somewhat, but it still remains the only eminence with a remotely mountainous summit for miles around. A large cave here, Denny's Hole, contained a mosaic of fragile encrustations, but a gruff-voiced tribe, clad in boiler-suits, thick boots and carbide lamps, appropriated these sparklers. Ghastly Morlocks of this sort are, apparently, common throughout all limestone regions of the British Isles.

Culbone Church. A photogenic little place of worship. Measuring 33 feet long by 12 wide, it is said to be the smallest church in Britain. Predominantly Gothic, the foundation of this fabric can be traced back to Saxon times, the font being Norman. Tucked coyly away in a leafy valley, an impressive annual output of postcards celebrate its fetching appearance and situation. The registers start at 1686.

Curry Rivel. In this parish, on a hill summit, is Burton Steeple: a plain Doric column designed by Capability Brown for William Pitt, Earl of Chatham, in memory of William Pynsent. In 1948, an adventurous cow, magnetised by this obelisk, managed to struggle up the spiral staircase to the top. There, struck with vertigo, the hapless brute staggered and swayed, and, finally, crashed to its death over the edge of the parapet.

Ditcheat. The Holy Well, a petrifying spring, lies outside this village.

Downside Abbey. The tower of the Benedictine Abbey here attains a height of 166 feet, higher than any other in the country, excluding Wells.

Dundry Hill. This outcrop, 764 feet high and composed of Oolitic Limestone, is crowned by an astronomical observatory; also, at its eastern extremity is Maes Knoll Tump, a large tumulus, 390 feet long and 45 feet high. Overlooking the village of Whitchurch, Hautville's Quoit stands securely-rooted in the turf. This large circular stone was, according to legend, used as a discus by Sir John de Hautville. For the palaeontologist, the area is rich in fossils of the Nautili-Ammonite kind.

Dunster. Above the much-photographed street and Yarn Market, but below the heftily-buttressed castle, is a shell tower, ivyclad and circular, with excellent views. Built for Henry Fownes Luttrell in 1775, this landmark has served Bristol Channel navigators well.

East Cranmore. On a high hill above this parish is a tower, erected in 1862 by J. M. Paget esq., a stark wind-bitten folly ascended by a spiral staircase.

East Harptree. Occupying a wooded glen near this village are the remains of Richmont Castle. In 1138 it was garrisoned by Sir William de Harptree who supported the claim of Henry I's daughter, Matilda, opposing the authority of King Stephen. However, by cunning strategy, fire and scaling ladders, the King secured mastery of the fortress and had it partially demolished.

Emborough Pool. In bad weather, this mere is supposed to strike the traveller with foreboding and dread, but it is, in actual fact, an attractive stretch of water, with its plantations of firs, beeches and sycamores. Locals declare it to occupy the vent of an old volcano.

Englishcombe. On the Bath–Wells road, this parish has twin yew trees, one of which flowers, and an ancient Tithe Barn.

Falkland. The village stocks are still standing on the green.

Farleigh Hungerford Castle: Sir Thomas Hungerford, tiring of the modest dimensions of his manor house, reinstated his family in this grandiloquent shell. There is a large rectangular inner court retaining two of its original four towers; the outer court encloses the family chapel and tombs.

Flax Bourton. A primitive carving on the tympanium of the parish church depicts St Michael brutalising a dragon with a beaded tail His cross protrudes from the poor beast's throat like a gigantic thermometer.

Frome. Once the centre of a prosperous cloth industry, this large market town has numerous fine seventeenth-and eighteenth-century houses (Cork Street and Willow Vale), a fourteenth-century bridge (Murty's Bridge), Cheap Street, a cobbled highway for pedestrians only, and the parish church of St John, built in the Decorated and Early English styles with the reredos carved in Carara marble, representing the 'Last Supper', the 'Striking of the Rock by Moses', and the 'Children of Israel gathering Manna in the Wilderness'. Bishop Ken, who was deprived of the See of Bath and Wells by William III, is buried in the churchyard.

Glastonbury. Venerated as the 'Mystic Avalon' of King Arthur, the shrine of the early Christians, the town that inspired John Cowper Powys to write probably the most charged and sensuous masterpiece in the English language ('A Glastonbury Romance')—Glastonbury is a must for scholars and solemn young transcendentalists, who, aligning the Tor with the pyramids and zodiac signs, declare it to be one of the great 'power centres' of the ancient world. For this we must partly blame John Michell, author of a number of esoteric works. The Abbey ruins, washed by centuries of rain and tinted with lichen, exude a delicate poetry of decay. Joseph of Arimithea, according to legend, visited this spot and founded the first religious house. The Holy Thorn, on Wirral Hill, was believed to have sprung from his staff, but was destroyed in the Civil War. A thorn in the abbey grounds is said to be a cutting from it. The town is, of course, wholly puffed-out with Arthurian associations; the dying monarch was ferried here to be healed of his grievous wound, to the island-vale of Avalon, the Anglo-Saxon lotos land, mild, sweet and lushly pastoral. Curiously enough, the word 'avlon' in Saxon means 'apple'. Probably, in pagan fertility rituals, apple-juice or cider played a special role.

Goathurst. In Halswell Park, a magnificent mansion dating from the Tudor period, are grounds where Romanticism achieved its fullest expression; for they contained Robin Hood's Temple, an eerie partially-collapsed structure in bark, a Rotunda, a Temple with an Ionic portico and flanking columns, and an Equestrian Sarcophagus with garlands at its base, celebrating the prowess of a noble filly, or stallion, who died after winning a hard race. There is also a Stepped Pyramid touchingly inscribed to a pure nymph. The shattered remnants of these may only be inspected today.

Hatch Beauchamp. In the Church of St John the Baptist is a memorial to commemorate Colonel Chard, V.C., the gallant defender of Rourkes Drift (January 22nd, 1879) during the Zulu War. Later this incident formed the substance of the film 'Zulu', starring Stanley Baker and Michael Caine.

Hemington. A definite eye-catcher in this parish is Ammerdown Park Column, a 180 feet tower built for Lord Hylton in 1865. The glass lantern at the top is reached by ascending an iron staircase; the base of the column is decorated with antique statues. Turner's Tower, about two miles distant, is an Italianate rejoinder to this architectural aberration, but is today in ruins.

Horwood. At Physicwell House is a well, 11 feet deep, containing medicinal salts.

Kingston Seymour. A modern sewage plant, opened here recently, strains human and chemical waste through PVC filters and distribution pipes with spray nozzles.

Long Ashton. A immense brooding shell of a building, Ashton Court is 300 feet long, with a gatehouse and traces of Baroque and Elizabethan work in the interior.

Lundy Island. Impressive precipitous island rising out of the sea like a huge stone gull. Puffins, guillemots, razorbills and peregrine falcons may be seen here, along with grey Atlantic seals, wild goats, deer and Soay sheep. The granite surface of the island is littered with fantastic rock formations, and its history, fraught with tales of piracy, war and escaped convicts, is equally exciting. More recently, Evelyn Waugh, in his posthumously published diaries, describes a lurid party he attended here in scandalous detail.

Mells. A five-gabled Elizabethan Manor House, rural cottages, and a church with a richly-decorated tower, some Jacobean pews and a plaque designed by Burne-Jones (a peacock on a tomb), feature among the attractions of this highly-praised village. The nursery-rhyme, 'Little Jack Horner', has somewhat spuriously been construed as referring to the former lords of this manor. Kilmersdon, a fine neglected village—grave, dignified, with a beautiful church and old lock-up called the Blind House—is worth examining, too. Coleford, in the same parish, has a church in which members of the Scott family are buried. The great explorer is duly saluted—'And in memory of Robert Falcon Scott, C.V.O., Captain, R.N., who, in returning from the South Pole with his companions, was translated by a glorious death in March, 1912.'

Mendip Lodge. At the east end of Dolebury Warren sprawls this luxurious ruin. Built by Dr Whalley, son of a Regius Professor of Divinity, this grandiose show place mansion once had an 84 feet long Italian verandah and fifty-two grottoes in its grounds. De Quincey, who derided the whole project, described it as being furnished by vast china jars and other knickknackery baubles. Only sagging, weed-strangled dilapidation is left today—but it still exudes a chilling atmosphere.

Midford Castle. This splendid mansion—one of the loveliest in the county—was built at the request of Henry Woolhouse Roeback to dissipate his gambling profits. The plan of the house, allegedly, was based on an Ace of Spades. Nearby, the Priory, now derelict, with Gothic windows and collapsed tower, dates from 1780.

Milverton. At Olands, a large mansion in this parish, a quantity of Roman coins were found in an urn (1847). They belonged to the reigns of Faustina (A.D. 125–175); Julian (360–3); Valentinian I, Valens and Valentinian II (364–97); Theodosius Maximus (370–95) and Arcadius (395–408). In 1773, the scientist and Egyptologist, Thomas Young, was born here. He is credited with being the founder of physiological optics and was one of the first to interpret the hieroglyphics on the Rosetta Stone.

Minehead. As at Padstow, this small town bursts into life each May Day and parades its Obby Oss: a ghastly phallic brute, bedecked with coloured discs, streaming ribbons and a tin mask. According to the gifted Cornish writer Donald Rawe, 'Minehead's horse is apt to become mischievous, rushing at onlookers and swinging round to strike them with his tail.' The custom has its origin in the ancient fertility rites, the stallion or the 'Oss' being regarded a synonymous with potency and virility.

Muchelney Abbey. A tradition states that Athelstan, King of England, after dirtying his hands by involving himself in the murder of Edward Atheling (A.D. 937), founded this Benedictine establishment as an act of penitence. The cloisters, refectory, kitchen and abbot's lodging-house remains in a good state of preservation.

Nailsea. A town once noted for its vivid and sometimes streakily-patterned glassware and coal pits, both of which are now abandoned. Nailsea Court, a well-kept manor house, successfully integrates Elizabethan and later styles; the Dorset poet, William Barnes, was married at the parish church. It is today a place where the new has swamped the old, a straggling street, subwayed, prosperous, with good modern shops, garages and a handful of older buildings. Housing estates, like huge rectangular blisters, mysteriously edge into the green fields beyond.

Nempnett Thrubwell. Outside this village, overgrown with ash trees, briars and thick shrubs, stands the Fairy's Toot, formerly one of the most awe-inspiring burial mounds in the British Isles. Originally this chambered tumulus, measuring 60 yards long by about 20 broad and 15 high, comprised a mass of rubble upheld by a wall, the intervening space being filled by two rows of cells separated by vast stone slabs. A great pile of human bones and horses' teeth were found here, but, with true countrymen's reverence for irreplaceable archaeological relics, they were fed into a lime-kiln and the tumulus was gradually dismantled. Little remains today, but it is said to retain a capacity for curing warts and similar protrusions.

North Curry. Until 1841 the Reeve's Feast used to be enacted here. One aspect of this ancient custom dictated that, on Boxing Day, a lavish feast was laid out in honour of King John, an effigy of him being placed on the table, presiding over an enormous mince pie. Eating, drinking and proclaiming toasts to his majesty would then continue uninterrupted until two Illb candles were burnt out. A full account of this ritualised celebration is inscribed on a tablet in the vestry of the parish church.

Nunney Castle. This solid compact structure, during the Civil War, withstood only two days siege before falling to the Parliamentarians. Engirdled by a moat and with substantial angle towers, it was built by Sir John de la Mare in 1373 and has been compared to the Bastille. The walls are 7 feet thick in places; the moat is 20 feet broad by 10 feet deep.

Nynehead Court. The River Tone here clatters over a fine series of cascades in the ornamental gardens.

Penselwood. On the London–Exeter road. In this parish are Pen Pits, an expanse of shafts and filled-in hollows which have been variously identified as ancient pit-dwellings, storage cavities and refugee camps for British women and children during the Roman conquest. Lieutenant-General A. H. L. Fox-Pitt-Rivers, F.R.S., F.S.A., picking them over with scholarly astuteness in 1883, pronounced them as quarries for querns (stone hand-mills for corn), a verdict which, in the light of recent research, is improbable.

Portbury. Formerly an important parish, Portbury has disclosed extensive Roman remains, villas, roads and coins. Conygar Hill, nearby, is crowned by an Iron Age camp. The Priory here, ashlar-faced and partly-restored, has an angle tower.

Priston Mill. This corn mill, about $5\frac{1}{4}$ miles south-west of Bath, is listed in the Domesday Book and is powered by a large overshot water wheel. Rebuilt in 1750, it is still in use today.

Sedgemoor. In 1685 Charles II died and was succeeded by the Roman Catholic Duke of York (James I). The Protestant Duke of Monmouth, illegitimate son of Charles II, invaded the West Country and was defeated at Sedgemoor: a level peaty expanse traversed by a huge drain. Monmouth supporters were brutally dealt with at Judge Jeffreys' Bloody Assize. At Norton St Phillip is the George Inn, an outstanding example of fifteenth-century architecture, where the Duke slept shortly before his disastrous engagement.

Severn Bridge. Opened in 1966, this suspension bridge is the seventh longest in the world (3,240 feet): a graceful arrangement of ferro-concrete affording swift access to the Wye Valley and the Welsh tribes. Upstream the Severn Bore is occasionally observed. This tidal wave occurs when the incoming water flows on top of the river and produces a wave sometimes attaining a height of six feet. It is seen to best advantage between Awre and Gloucester during the high equinoctial tides (February–April and August–October).

Shepton Mallet. Two unexplained disappearances diversify the history of this market town and manufacturing centre. One of them concerns Nancy Camel, a gargoyle-visaged old crone who wandered about the streets of Shepton with her donkey and cart. The other more reliably documented disappearance took place in 1763 and is recorded in some detail by Collinson. Owen Parfitt, an invalided tailor who had, in his younger days, served as a soldier in the American army—was a dwindling shadow of a man. He depended solely on the care lavished on him by his elderly sister. She would carry him downstairs and leave him in the passageway of their house, so that he might derive the benefit of the fresh air. One evening she left him in this posture and returned minutes later to find him gone. He was never seen or heard of again. In the Unitarian Chapel there is an elaborate pulpit and a tablet to Stephen Browne, theologian, author and preacher. After losing his wife and son—coupled with the accidental shooting of a highwayman who tried to rob him—this distinguished Nonconformist divine began to behave oddly and be oppressed by feelings of worthlessness. He would proclaim aloud that he was a 'contemptible beast'; that God had annihilated the 'thinking substance' of his mind, and that all his fluent sermons contained as little sense as a parrot's burblings.

Simonsbath. The dour little capital of Exmoor.

South Cadbury. Traditionally the Camelot of King Arthur, this impressive hill fort with a perimeter of 1,200 yards may have once accommodated a very large striking force of men. Leslie Alcock, director of excavations, reports uncovering a large timber feasting-hall and a sturdy gate-tower. The King himself, accompanied by the jingling of ghostly spurs and the baying of hounds, still hunts around these parts.

Spaxton. Following the example of H. J. Prince, the Rev. J. H. Smyth-Pigott caused a nation-wide sensation when he announced himself as a Messiah and revived the 'Agapeonites' in this small village. Coming of a good Somerset family he had been ordained by the Bishop of London in 1883 and promoted himself to a Divinity in 1902 at the 'Church of the Ark of the Covenant' in Clapton, London. His antics and the numerous women attracted to his cause made lively scandal in the early years of this century. A short, thin-featured man, with dark glowing eyes and pince-nez, Smyth-Pigott had lived a varied life as a seaman, coffee-planter, university man and soldier. In 1909 he was found guilty of immorality, uncleanness and wickedness of life. 'I am God,' he defended himself. 'It does not matter what they do to me. There is no such thing as marriage in the Agapeone. We are all brothers and sisters in God.' The Messiah, despite his claims to the contrary, died in March 1927, wearied, sad, resigned to the world's indifference and contempt. He is Somerset's gentle rival to Warwickshire's Aleister Crowley.

Stanton Drew. This parish, on the River Chew, has several clusters of standing stones, some arranged in circles, some lying flat, some remaining upright and forming avenues. Once these were thought to commemorate the eleventh battle fought by King Arthur during his journey from Caerleon-on-Usk to Badon Hill, but there is a legend stating that they were a group of dancers who were metamorphosed by the Devil. There is also a superstition accompanying their removal or tampering-with in any way. According to Wood: 'No one, say the country people about Stantondrue, was ever able to reckon the number of these metamorphosed stones, or to take a draught of them, though several have attempted to do both, and proceeded till they were either dead upon the spot, or struck with such an illness as soon carried them off.' In actual fact the precise number of stones can be easily added up: one of the circles has 14; another 6; another—

Stavordale. In 1904, F. C. Sage, esq. purchased the ancient Augustinian Priory here and set about restoration work. Founded by the Lovells in the thirteenth century and dedicated to St James, the building houses a nave, choir, and a fine chapel with a fan-traceried roof.

Stoke Lane Slocker. A remarkable cave situated near the village of Stoke Lane on the Mendips. Anyone willing to crawl about for long periods in a cold stream—gurgling along claustrophobic and murky passages—and immerse himself under a series of sumps, will be rewarded by the sight of some beautiful calcite formations. In 1963, a Bristol University lecturer, by his devotion to this sombre task, contracted Weil's disease, an infection fairly well-known among sewage workers.

Taunton. The county town of Somerset, Taunton offers a variety of attractions: Taunton Castle and County Museum, established A.D. 710, with a Norman keep and Great Hall (scene of Bloody Assize); Gray's Almhouses, a group of red-brick buildings dating from 1635; St Margaret's Hospital, founded originally for the treatment of lepers; Shire Hall, with busts of celebrated Somerset personalities in the entrance hall; the Military Museum and Vivary Park, laid out with streams, gardens, a model boatpond and recreational facilities. Clatworthy, in the nearby Brendon Hills, is a well-stocked trout fishery.

Watchet. Bright red conglomerate and pale green limestone stripe the cliffs around this small port. Alabaster is sometimes worked in the region of Blue Anchor Bay which also boasts a Coastal Waterfall.

Wells. According to tradition, the first church was founded here by King Ine in A.D. 705. The present Cathedral—considered by some the best example to be found in the whole world of a secular church with its subordinate buildings, has a west front embellished with 400 statues of saints, angels and prophets. A climb to the top of the tower is an excellent way to appreciate the layout of the medieval town. The Vicar's Close—one of the oldest streets in Europe—blurrs one's sense of time and identity, and the lovely Bishop's Palace, surrounded by a wide moat, might have come straight out of Mallory.

Wookey Hole. Under a craggy forehead of a cliff, the subterranean River Axe emerges from the jaws of this eerie, colour-daubed cavern. Excavation of the cave-floor has unearthed daggers, knives, pottery, coins, spindle whorls, weaving combs and objects of craftsmanship in silver and bronze. Divers, working upstream, have identified some dozen additional chambers. Alexander Pope, to furnish his Hampstead Grotto, ordered soldiers to shoot stalactities off the cave-roof.

The Hyena Den, on the east side of the valley, has disclosed bones of mammoth, rhinoceros, hyena, lion and rodent, together with implements belonging to Pleistocene Man. The Ebbor Gorge, in the immediate vicinity, a lonely and rugged cleft, is a satisfyingly desolate stroll—now adapted as a Nature Trail.

Wraxall. Architect, John Norton, enlarged Tyntesfield House into what it is today, a gloomy, spikily impressive Gothic residence, with a huge chapel and a square tower.

Wrington. Hannah More, novelist and philanthropist, lived in this mellow village. The Church of All Saints has a spectacular tower, of two stages, with a recessed and panelled west doorway and a large window of six lights. John Locke, the philosopher, founder of empiricism, was born in a nearby cottage (now fallen down). He is mainly remembered for his 'Essay on Human Understanding', the type of work intellectual bluffers mention respectfully rather than read.

Yatton. A straggling market town with a good church and a mainline railway station.

Yeovil. This ancient borough and market town has an impressive Town Hall, built in the Italian style, the front of which displays six pillars supporting a frieze and cornice; also, the church of St John the Baptist, dating from the middle of the fourteenth century, and Sidney Gardens, laid out with a bandstand, fountains and seats. Barwick Park, nearby, however, is more interesting, for it boasts a series of refreshingly eccentric follies: the Cone, a stark and startling 75 feet spire; the Needle, a crudely-assembled pile of stones shaped as its name implies; the Fish Tower, a plainish column 50 feet tall; Jack the Treacle Eater, an arch and tower, topped by the statue of Mercury and named after a local runner who trained on treacle, or, alternatively, of a murderer who hid in the nearby tower and was fed with sandwiches containing this glutinous substance. The most blood-freezing and sinister of all grottoes is, in the opinion of Barbara Jones, to be seen in these grounds: 'a huge cold vault smelling of sour earth, with earth in the thick air and earth in the jagged stones . . .'

Yeovilton, to the north, has a Fleet Air Arm base. Visitors may climb into the cockpits of RAF Phantoms and imagine themselves within an earlier prototype, alert, moustachioed, spruce as Kenneth More, depositing their hardware on the citizens of Dresden to the strains of obligatory patriotic music. A museum, illustrating the history of flying from 1910 to the present day, occupies one of the hangars.

LITERARY NOTE

A NUMBER of distinguished writers were either born in Somerset or else resided there for a considerable period. One of England's finest picaresque novelists, Henry Fielding, author of 'Tom Jones', was born at Sharpham near Glastonbury in 1707. Sydney Smith, Canon of St Paul's and conspicuous wit, held from 1829 until his death the living of Combe Florey. A less revered, but intellectually formidable economist and politician, Walter Bagehot, was born at Langport and wrote 'The English Constitution', one of the most penetrative assessments of its kind ever published. The Reverend John Langharne, D.D., joint translator with his brother, William, of 'Plutarch's Lives', was rector in the parish of Blagdon from 1767 to 1769, and the poet, William Wordsworth, while Coleridge was living at Nether Stowey, stayed at Alfoxton House, near Holford, in the Quantock Hills.

Yet it does seem, on the face of it, that names of certain authors of genius have imprinted themselves more deeply upon the character of some towns than others. Possibly, while they were actually there, they were ignored or dismissed as effete scribblers, but in later years, after posterity has crowned their brows with laurels and adverse critics been consumed in the brightening blaze of their reputation, the towns they were born at, or were glancingly associated with, have grasped them to their bosoms and boasted of their association in numerous guidebooks.

Bath is, of course, the town with the most impressive literary track record, but its associations are too numerous and well known to be dealt with here. Suffice to say, as a centre of fashion it was frequented by such polished individuals as the young Sheridan, Beau Brummel, and seething hordes of Regency bucks and braggarts. Jane Austen, in her last novel 'Persuasion', casts her sharp but unsentimental eye over its latter-day pretensions, and the figure of William Beckford, the last of the great Romantic eccentrics, lends it a slightly more sinister dimension.

A far less fashionable spot, Clevedon, has done remarkably well out of those frail coincidences which link eminent men of letters with specific locations. Samuel Taylor Coleridge started the ball rolling by bringing his young wife, Sara Fricker, to a cottage here and fluting prettily:

> Low was our pretty cot—our tallest rose
> Peep'd at the chamber window. We could hear
> At silent noon and eve and early morn,
> The sea's faint murmur . . .

It is depressing to reflect that, despite its lyrical beginnings, Coleridge's marriage to Sara never really worked out. Her mind proved of a more prosaic cast than he, in the first flush of love, had ever anticipated. His deepest obsessions, understandably, left her unmoved. For reasons not hard to fathom, German metaphysics, labyrinthine mystical and theological speculations, advanced notions of forming pantisocracies, and all the other lumber stockpiled in the brilliant junkshop of her husband's mind, found no place in her straightforward feminine personality. She was as simple as he was complex.

The 'cot' at which they honeymooned is ostensibly in Old Church Road, opposite the Curzon Cinema, but the criteria upon which this site was finally established is oral rather than documentary. Lady Elton, quashing the fragile claims of the smaller building at the west end of the town, decreed this red-tiled cottage to be the scene of Coleridge's nuptials, and, despite the presence of other contenders, thus it has remained. Today the building wears its plaque with invincible authority. Quite rightly, too. Although its identity has been disputed, it has the longest tradition of being 'Coleridge Cottage', and, as far back as 1838, sketches of it were being sold at a bazaar under that very title. At that time Coleridge's confidant and friend, Joseph Cottle, a Bristol poet and bookseller, was alive and well—and he never questioned the authenticity of these sketches (though, admittedly, he may never have seen them). So perhaps the claims of 'Coleridge Cottage' are sounder than some may think.

Tennyson and Thackeray also have connections with the town. It is popularly asserted that the novelist, who had friends at the Court and often stayed there, introduced it as the 'Castlewood' of his novel, 'Henry Esmond', although the description of the two residences far from tally. Thackeray's friend, Mrs Brookfield, whose maiden name was Jane Octavia Elton, is sometimes acknowledged as the original of Lady Castlewood.

Thackeray apart, another excellent novelist, George Gissing, introduces Clevedon into his novel, 'The Odd Women'. Although the town is never realised in precise visual terms, it looms beyond the harrowing emotional conflicts of the story as a haven of bourgeois quietude. A pathetic faith in the curative properties of saltwater and sea air is implicit in fragments of the dialogue. One character is heard to remark—'It's only this cursed London that has come between us. At Clevedon we shall begin our lives over again—like we did at Guernsey. All our trouble, I am convinced, has come of ill-health.'

Arthur Hallam, object of much posthumous eulogising, was the grandson of Sir Abraham Elton and is buried in St Andrew's Church. Tennyson's poem 'In Memoriam', by turns gloomy and duskily sensuous, bitterly laments his passing:

> He is not here; but far away
>   The noise of life begins again,
> And ghastly thro' the drizzling rain
>   On the bald street breaks the blank day.

The tragedy of Hallam's death to his contemporaries was one of unfulfilled promise. Like Keats, he was abruptly snuffed out in the bright flame of his youth, but, unlike the latter, we are left with no solid evidence of his abilities, only the tears and flowery tributes to the nobleness of his demeanour, the stateliness of his countenance, the dignified grace of his bearing—phrases that might as well refer to a marble statue of Prince Albert. His epitaph, predictably, conforms to this vein, being an extravagant Victorian panegyric—'And now in this obscure and solitary church repose the mortal remains of one too early lost for public fame, but already conspicuous among his contemporaries for the brightness of his genius, the depth of his understanding, the nobleness of his disposition, the fervour of his piety, and the purity of his life.' No doubt, somewhere beyond the veils of verbiage, the grim and grandly-phrased funeral orations, a real and charming Arthur Hallam existed.

Nevertheless, the Hallam-Tennyson connection is one of the most consistently evoked in regard to Clevedon Church, and poets who visit the town tend to scribble a few obligatory lines to Alfred and Arthur. That once grand, but now almost forgotten, literary despot, Andrew Lang, visited the church and dashed off a lyric which could be regarded as a sort of pendant to 'In Memoriam':

> Westward I watch the low blue hills of Wales,
>   The low sky silver grey:
> The turbid Channel with its scattered sails
>   Mourns through the winter day.
> There is no colour but one ashen light;
>   On shore and hill and lea;
> The little Church beneath the grassy height
>   Is grey as sky or sea.
> But there hath he, who won the sleepless love
>   Slept for these fifty years;
> There is the grave that hath been wept above
>   With more than mortal tears.
> And far below you hear the Channel weep,
>   And all his waves complain,—
> As Hallam's dirge through all the years must keep
>   Its monotone of pain!

A far more obscure literary figure, T. E. Brown, Manxman and fellow of Oriel College, also left a poetic snapshot of the Channel at Clevedon in an image worthy of T. E. Hulme or Pound:

> The sea was Lazarus, all day
> At Dives gate he lay,
> And lapped the crumbs.
> Night comes;
> The beggar dies—
> Forthwith the Channel, coast to coast
> Is Abraham's bosom; and the beggar lies
> A lovely ghost.

Yet another songbird, Rupert Brooke, visited Clevedon briefly during the early part of this century. His impression of the resort is less lyrical than those of his forbears; he describes it as a 'dreadful place' and complains that the barber will not cut his hair on Saturdays.

A less glamorous, but no less deserving poet, William Lisle Bowles, is associated with Weston-super-Mare. He was the son of the rector of Uphill and later Canon of Salisbury Cathedral. In the opinion of Austin Dobson, it was the 'candle of Bowles that lit the fire of Coleridge', his finest work being his sonnets, first published in 1789. His other compositions are less successful: 'Stick to thy sonnets, Bowles,—at least they pay'—was the dismissive rebuff of Byron. In old age, when desire and health were failing, he returned to Weston and would stroll along the beach ruefully meditating on the passage of the years and humanity's joyless lot. These lines, poignant and life-weary, were composed shortly before his death in 1850.

> Was it but yesterday I heard the roar
> Of these white coursing waves, and trod the shore,
> A young and playful child—but yesterday?
> Now I return with locks of scattered grey,
> And wasted strength; for many, many years
> Have passed, some marked by joy and some by tears,
> Since we last parted. As I gaze around
> I think of time's fleet step, that makes no sound.
>
> In yonder vale, beneath the hill top tower,
> My father decked the village pastor's bower;*
> Now he and all beneath whose knees I played,
> Cold in the narrow cell of death are laid.
> 'My father,' to the lonely surge I sigh;
> 'My father,' the lone surge seems to reply;
> Yet the same shells and seaweeds seem to strew
> The sandy margin as when life was new.

---

* He planted the Parsonage gardens at Uphill.

> I mourn not time's inevitable tide,
> Whose swift career ten thousand feel beside;
> I mourn not for the days that are no more,
> But come a stranger, Weston, to thy shore
> In search of health alone, and woo the breeze
> That wander o'er thy solitary seas;
> To chase the mist with these oppressed eyes,
> And renovate life's languid energies.

Weston, as a holiday shrine, also attracted the vivacious Mrs Piozzi. Friend and confidant of Dr Johnson during his blackest moments, she was a highly regarded figure in that small literary coterie in which he was the dominant member. She nursed him through severe bouts of insanity and was for a long period his keeper; the break came when she married the aimiable Piozzi, who was several years younger than herself, and entered into a new phase of life. This attractive and likeable woman succumbed enthusiastically to the allurements of Weston; in 1819, she wrote to Sir James Fellows, her physician, comparing the 'gridiron' and 'stewpot' conditions of Bath unfavourably with the more bracing aspect of Weston: 'The breezes here are most salubrious; no land nearer than North America when we look at the Channel; and 'tis said that Sebastian Cabot used to stand where I sit and meditate his future discoveries of Newfoundland. I inquired for books. "There are but two," was the reply: a Bible and Paradise Lost. They were the best, however. No market, but I didn't care about that.'

A very different place, East Coker, has become a place of pilgrimage for the literati since T. S. Eliot, the Anglo-American poet, was buried here—the hamlet from which his forbears originally sprung. This author, whose early work excited and inspired his followers as much as his later verse-sermonising alienated some of them, is regarded as the most influential of the century. The tablet inscribed to him in the parish church is simple, moving and forceful.

The village was also the birthplace of William Dampier (1652–1715), explorer, circumnavigator, author of 'A New Voyage Round the World' and 'A Discourse on Winds'. The latter, a seminal mariner's text, is still said to have value today.

Dampier, who made a voyage to Newfoundland at the age of sixteen, lived a dynamic and turbulent life, and, while working as an assistant manager of a plantation in Jamaica, was suspected of being in league with pirates. Large tracts of Australia, groups of islands and parts of the New Guinea coast, bear his name today; and his birthplace, a low, thatched building with Gothic windows, is one of East Coker's most revered features. Apart from being a brilliant sailor, Dampier was indirectly responsible for one of England's earliest adventure stories. During one of his voyages, Andrew Selkirk, believing Dampier's vessel to be unsafe, asked to be left ashore on a desert island. His subsequent adventures were fictionalised in Daniel Defoe's 'Robinson Crusoe'.

Another distinguished wanderer and historian, Alexander Kinglake (1809–91), was born at Taunton. He made his mark with the publication of 'Eothen' in 1844. This narrative of Eastern travel has been reissued many times and continues to sell today in paperback, while his magnum opus, 'Invasion of the Crimea'—eight volumes of fanatically painstaking research—gathers dust in library vaults and second-hand bookshops.

An early and now-neglected literary figure, Samuel Daniel (1562–1619), also hailed from Taunton. A contemporary of William Shakespeare, he was appointed the equivalent to poet-laureate in 1599 (the official title had not been established then) and produced pastorals, sonnets, tragedies, and a 'History of England', till the time of Edward III. His great poem, 'The History of the Civil Wars between the Houses of York and Lancaster', despite its metrical facility and rhetorical panache, graces the pages of no contemporary volume. His bust, in the Classical manner, may be inspected in Beckington Church.

Finally, it would be an affront not to treat at some length that genial eccentric, Thomas Coryate, author of 'Crudities' and 'Coryat's Crambe or Colwort Twice Sodden'. This remarkable traveller was born at the parish of Odcombe in 1577, and after years of wandering in Europe, Asia Minor, Persia and India, died at Surat in 1617. Many of his expeditions were undertaken on foot, and, like an earlier 'Walking Stewart',* he was a recognised figure in the literary coteries of the day, acting as a butt or foil to the wits with whom he associated.

Coryate's most remarkable quality was his courage. He would venture into dangerous bandit-infested regions accompanied only by immense fund of self-esteem. His character, in some ways, was almost touchingly naive. A devout and assertive Christian, he was occasionally pompous and bombastic towards intelligent followers of alien creeds, but conversely, he could also be warm, humorous, adaptable, and capable of absorbing social and cultural customs of other lands with ease and naturalness.

A quaint aspect of his character was his penchant for making speeches. He took great pride in his masterly command of English, and was always glad if granted the opportunity to declaim an oration before a distinguished or high-ranking personage. These addresses were often remarkable compositions. If directed towards an English audience, they were inevitably vehicles fashioned to transport the most rarefied and orchidaceous words his considerable erudition could muster. If, on the other hand, they were composed with an eye to loosening the purse-strings of a Shah or Sultan, they were clear and comprehensible enough. His address to Jahangir, the Great Mogul, supreme ruler of vast tracts of North India and Asia, is a model of elegant obsequity:

> Lord Protector of the World, all haile to you. I am a poore traveller and world-seer, which am come hither from a farre country, namely England, which auncient historians thought to have been situated in the farthest bounds of the West, and which is the queene of all the ilands in the world. The cause of my coming hither is for foure respects. First, to see the blessed face of Your Majesty, whose wonderfull fame hath resounded all over Europe and the Mahotmetan countries; when I heard of the fame of Your Majesty, I hastened hither with speed, and travelled very cheerfully

---

* See De Quincey's essay on John Stewart.

to see your glorious court. Secondly, to see Your Majesties elephants, which kind of beasts I have not seen in any other country. Thirdly, to see your famous river Ganges, which is the captaine of all the rivers of the world. The fourth is this: to intreat Your Majesty that you would vouchsafe to grant mee your gracious passe that I may travell into the country of Tartaria to the city of Samarcand, to visit the blessed sepulcher of the Lord of the Corners, whose fame, by reason of his warres and victories is published over the whole world ... These foure causes moved me to come out of my native country thus farre, having travelled a foote through Turky and Persia. So farre have I traced the world into this country that my pilgrimage hath accomplished three thousand miles; wherein I have sustained much labour and toile, the like whereof no mortall man in this world did ever performe, to see the blessed face of Your Majesty since the first day you were inaugurated in your glorious monarchall throne.

For this rather magnificent essay in public relations, the Emperor casually tossed a hundred silver rupees into a suspended silken sheet, which Coryate, although he was hoping for a much larger sum, gratefully accepted. What does testify to his sheer intelligence and application, however, is the fact that the oration quoted was declaimed in Persian, the translation being Coryate's own. He could absorb the essential elements of diverse tongues, such as Hindu and the Levantine languages, with incredible facility.

His friend, the Reverend Terry, wrote a pertinent assessment of his virtues and failings as a man and a writer. Initially he praises Coryate's veracity, drawing attention to the fact that he was a faithful recorder of what he heard and saw. He did not—a favourite trick of early travel writers—go peopling unexplored parts of the globe with fabulous semi-mythical monsters, secure in the belief that none of his readers would be able to contradict his testimony. Indeed paucity of material posed no problem to Coryate; he had no need to invent. His books are ponderous padded-out affairs, floridly-written, displaying a wide range of learning.

Terry, more curiously, indicates that Coryate's obsession with travel was not an end in itself, but rather he regarded it as a means whereby he could gain distinction and the admiration of others. His failing, in brief, was that he was a swank—'He was a man who had got the mastery of many hard languages ... But his knowledge and high attainments made him not a little ignorant of himself; he being so covetous, so ambitious of praise that he would hear and endure more of it than he could in any measure deserve; being like a ship that hath too much sail and too little ballast.' He adds, ruefully recalling the sneery versifiers and literary wiseacres of Coryate's London days—'Yet if he had not fall'n into the smart hands of the wits of those times, he might have passed better ... 'Twas fame, without doubt, that stirred up this man unto those voluntary but hard undertakings, and the hope of that glory which he should reap after he had finished his long travels made him not at all take notice of the hardships he found in them.'

He is perhaps being too stern a critic here. It could be said that most of England's great adventurers, men like Sir Richard Burton, Speke and T. E. Lawrence, had a strong streak of vanity in their character. To communicate what you see, what adventures you experience, and enjoy a measure of flattery and adulation, is only too human a failing, and Coryate, the first man to walk to India, the only reliable witness of the Mermaid Tavern meetings, the first traveller to examine in a scholarly fashion the sites of antiquity on the Trojan Plain, the friend of Ben Jonson, Inigo Jones, John Donne and Sir Thomas Roe, deserved his small reputation—for he used his time dynamically and resourcefully.

Winding up, Terry invokes the grim, but inescapable, truism that, whatever one makes of one's life, the great equaliser will raze it to the uncomplicated elemental level—'Sic exit Coryatus: Hence he went off the stage, and so must all after him, how long soever their parts seem to be: for if one should go to the extremest part of the world East, another West, another North, and another South, they must all meet together in the Field of Bones, wherein our traveller hath now taken his lodging, and where I leave him.'

No one knows where Coryate's true burial place is—a fact that would have sorely grieved the great traveller, but, by happy coincidence, a rather grand Mohammedan-style tomb a mile north of Surat, is called 'Tom Coryate's Tomb' and marked as such on the Admiralty maps. It is heartening to think that this larky, genial, swaggering Englishman, who was spurned and occasionally treated with cruel indifference by those who should have known better, has secured a place of immortality in a distant corner of Asia. There he lies—the Odcombian legge-stretcher, as he liked to dub himself—far from that tiny Somerset church where he once hung up his boots.

BIBLIOGRAPHY

REV. W. JACKSON: *Visitors' Handbook to Weston-super-Mare* (Hodder and Stoughton 1877)
GRAHAME FARR: *Somerset Harbours* (Christopher Johnson 1954)
EVE WIGAN: *Gordano* (most recent edition published by the Chatford House Press, Bristol 1971)
MICHAEL WILLIAMS: *The Draining of the Somerset Levels* (Cambridge University Press 1970)
J. S. HILL: *Somerset Names* (St Stephen's Press, Bristol 1913)
JOHN DUCK: *The Natural History of Portishead* (Evans and Abbot, Bristol 1852)
JOHN RUTTER: *Delineations of North-west Somerset* (Macmillan 1829)
THE REVEREND COLLINSON: *The History and Antiquities of the County of Somerset* (R. Cruttwell, Bath 1791)
FRANCIS KNIGHT: *The Seaboard of Mendip* (J. M. Dent 1902)
FRANCES HARIOTT: *Somerset Memories and Traditions* (Robert Scott: London MCMXXIV)
G. B. HARPER: *The Somerset Coast* (Chapman and Hall, London 1909)
Ward Lock's Guide to Weston-super-Mare
C. MAGGS: *The Weston, Clevedon and Portishead Light Railway* (Oakwood Press 1968)
GEORGE HENNING, M.D.: *An Historical Account of the Mineral Waters or Mineral Springs, at Burnham, Near Bridgwater* (George Aubrey, Bridgwater 1836)
BRYAN LITTLE: *Portrait of Somerset* (Robert Hale & Company, London 1969)

INDEX

A

Alfred the Great, 88, 89
Arden, John, 64
Arthur family, 24, 25, 54
Ashill, 108
Axbridge, 106

B

Banwell, 108
Barrow Gurney, 108, 109
Bath, 109
Bathford, 109
Becket, Thomas, 38, 39, 42, 91, 92
Beckford, William, 109, 119
Beckington, 109
Beechbarrow Farm, 109
Beerbohm, Max, 11
Berrow Flats, 71, 73
Berrow village, 74, 75
Bishop Ken, 30
Blackdown Hills, 107
Blagdon, 109
Bleadon, 60
Brean Down, 66, 67, 68, 102
Brean Leisure Centre, 71
Brean village, 68, 69
Brendon Hills, 107
Brent Knoll, 63, 65
Brett Young, Francis, 2
Bridgwater, 109
Bristol, 110
Bristol Corporation, 8, 9
Brockley Combe, 106
Brooke, Rupert, 122
Broomfield, 107
Brown, T. E., 122
Brush, Peter, 7
BURNHAM, 76–87; see also 93–101
    Catherine Terrace, 82, 83
    Clarence Hotel, 82
    Colony, the, 84, 85
    Custom House, 82
    Lifeboat Service, 81, 82
    Lighthouse, 79–81
    Queen's Hotel, 82, 83
    Saint Andrew's Church, 78, 79
    Saint Anne's, 84
    Stert House 83, 84
Burrow Bridge, 110
Butleigh Wootton, 110

C

Cadbury Camp, 13
Carmine, Timothy, 7
Castle Cary, 110
Cave, George, politician, 84
Chard, 110
Charterhouse, 105
Cheddar Gorge, 106
Chew Magna, 110
Christon, 110
Civil War, 3, 8, 19, 20
Clapton in Gordano, 24, 25, 26
Claverton, 110

Cleeve Abbey, 111
CLEVEDON, 10–18, 28, 29; see also 93–101
   All Saints' Church, 13
   Bandstand, 14
   Burstead House, 11, 12
   Christchurch, 12
   Church Hill, 14
   Clevedon Court, 15, 16
   Clocktower, 12, 16
   Council House, 12, 13
   Elton Road, 11, 17
   Fountain, Elton Road, 14
   Fountain, Pier Copse, 14
   Franciscan Friary, 17, 18
   Hale's Factory, 13
   Highdale Court, 12
   Ladye Bay, 20
   Mount Elton, 13
   Old Inn, 13
   Pier, the, 11
   Pier Toll House, 12
   Pill, the, 29
   Royal Pier Hotel, 12
   Saint Andrew's Church, 15
   Saint Antony's School, 12
   Saint Brandon's School, 14
   Saint Mary's Church, 19, 20
   Salthouse Hotel, 14
   Smugglers' Steps, 20
   Swiss Valley, 13
   Wain's Hill, 14, 28, 29
   Walton Castle, 20
Coke family, 8
Coleridge, S. T., poet, 120
Coryate, Thomas, 124–126
Cothelstone, 111
Crock, John, 40
Crook's Peak, 111
Crosse, Andrew, electrician, 107
Culbone Church, 111
Curry Rivel, 111

D

Dampier, William, 123
David Davies, Reverend, 76, 79, 80, 84
Ditcheat, 111
D'Orsay, Count, 11
Downside Abbey, 111
Dundry Hill, 111
Dunster, 111

E

East Brent, 64
East Cranmore, 111
East Harptree, 111
Eaton in Gordano, 26, 27

Eliot, T. S., 123
Elton family, 16, 33, 52
Elton Ware, 16
Emborough Pool, 112
Englishcombe, 112
Exmoor, 106, 107

F

Falkland, 112
Farleigh Hungerford, 112
Flatholm, 91, 92
Flax Bourton, 112
Frome, 112

G

Gildas, historian, 90
Gissing, George, 120
Glastonbury, 112
Goathurst, 112
Goblin Combe, 106
Goodere, Capt. Samuel, 3
Gordon, Squire, 9
Gytha, mother of Harold, 60

H

Hallam, Arthur, 121
Harper, C. G., 10, 20, 64
Hatch Beauchamp, 113
Hemington, 113
Highbridge, 89
Horwood, 113
Hubba, 58

J

James II, 3

K

Kenn, 29–33
Kent, Samuel Savile, 22
Kewstoke, 42
King, Doctor Walter, bishop, 79
Kinglake, Alexander, 123
Kingston Seymour, 32, 33, 113
Kipling, 1
Knyfton, Thomas, 60, 61

L

Lang, Andrew, 121
Lisle Bowles, William, 41, 122
Lloyd George, 12
Locke, Richard, 86, 87
Long Ashton, 113
Lundy Island, 113
Lympsham, 61, 62, 63

M

Mat Grass, 72
Mells, 113
Mendip Hills, 105, 106
Mendip Lodge, 113
Middle Hope, 39, 40, 101
Midford Castle, 114
Milverton, 114
Minehead, 114
Muchelney Abbey, 114
Monk's Steps, 42

N

Nailsea, 114
Nempnett Thrubwell, 114
Nettlecombe Church, 107
Nornen, 73
North Curry, 114
Nunney Castle, 115
Nynehead Court, 115

P

Parrett River, 87, 88
Penselwood, 115
Perceval family, 22, 23
Piozzi, Mrs Thrale, 123
Port, seafaring Saxon, 1
Portbury, 115
PORTISHEAD, 1–9, see also 93–101
  Battery Point, 2, 3, 101
  Black Nore Lighthouse, 6
  Boating Lake, 2
  Denny Island, 3
  Dock, the, 4, 5
  Dungball Island, 3
  Grange, the, 5
  Kingroad, 2
  Manor House, 6
  Market Cross, 9
  Millstone, the, 2, 5
  Nautical School, 2, 6
  Saint Mary's Church, 6
  Saint Mary's Well, 6
  White Lion, 2, 5
  Wireless Receiving and Transmitting Station, 7
  Woodhill Bay, 2
Poulett, Lord, 20
Priddy, 105
Priston Mill, 115
Ptolemy, 76

Q

Quantock Hills, 107

R

Ragwort, 72
Reed, George, 78, 83
Russell, Rev. C. D., 60

S

Saint Bridget, 69
Saint Lawrence, 36, 37
Samphire, 21
Sand Bay, 41, 42
Sea Buckthorn, 72
Sedgemoor, 115
Severn Bridge, 115
Shelduck, 66, 73, 74
Shepton Mallet, 115
Shiplate House, 61
Simonsbath, 116
Smyth-Pigott, Rev. J. H., 116
Somerset and Dorset Railway, 78
South Cadbury, 116
Spartina Grass, 71, 72
Spaxton, 116
Speke, John Hanning, 108
Spring Cove, 102
Stanton Drew, 116
Stavordale, 117
Steepholm, 90, 91
Stephenson, Rev. J. H. S., 62, 63
Stert Island, 87
Stoke Lane Slocker, 117
Swan, Diana, 106

T

Tarr Steps, 107
Taunton, 117
Tennyson, Alfred Lord, 120
Thackeray, W. M., 120
Toplady, Rev. Augustus, 105

U

Uphill, 58, 59, 102

W

Walton Bay Signal Station, 7
Walton in Gordano, 22
Walton Saint Mary's, 19, 20
Wansdyke, 1
Watchet, 117
Webbington, 61
Wellington, 107
Wells, 117
Weston, Clevedon and Portishead Light Railway, 34, 35
Weston in Gordano, 22, 23

129

Weston Moor Nature Reserve, 23
WESTON-SUPER-MARE, 45–55; see also 93–101
  Anchor Cove, 51
  Aquarium and Zoo, 49
  Birnbeck Pier, 51, 52
  Cemetery, 48
  Constitutional Club, 48
  Grand Pier, 49
  Grove Park, 48
  Knightstone, 51
  Lifeboat Service, 52, 53
  Model Village, 49
  Odean Cinema, 48
  Playhouse Theatre, 49
  Pool, the, 48, 49
  Punch and Judy, 45
  Regent Street, 50
  Royal Crescent, 48
  Saint John's Church, 48
  Town Hall, 48
  Waxworks, the, 50
  Winter Gardens, 48
Wick Saint Lawrence, 34–37
Willet's Tower, 107
Woodspring Priory, 38, 39
Wookey Hole, 117
Worle Observatory, 42
Worlebury Hill, 55, 56, 57
Worle village, 42, 43, 44
Wraxall, 117
Wrington, 117

Y

Yatton, 118
Yeo River, 33, 34
Yeovil, 118
Yeovilton, 118